ABSOLUT FOODING.
TBWA
ABSOLUT COUNTRY OF SWEDEN VODKA & LOGO, ABSOLUT, ABSOLUT BOTTLE DESIGN AND ABSOLUT CALLIGRAPHY ARE TRADEMARKS OWNED BY V&S VIN & SPRIT AB. © 2007 V&S VIN & SPRIT AB. PHOTO: MICHEL DUBOIS
absolut.com

Luxury
is
a
matter
of
how
much

BY MARGRIT GAUDARD

Luxus ist Raum erobern

Luxus geht auf Distanz zum schnöden Mammon. Denn Luxus wird, darin sind sich die Trendforscher einig, in Zukunft mehr und mehr immaterielle Züge annehmen. Bereits jetzt ist unser grösster Luxus die Zeit.

Ist die Heimat des Luxus der Orient? Sieht danach aus. Wenn König Fahd von Saudi-Arabien an den Gestaden des Genfersees in seiner 200-Millionen-Franken-Villa absteigt, ergiesst sich ein märchenhafter Goldsegen über die Calvin-Stadt. Der König aus dem Morgenland lässt die Münzen klingeln: Zwei Millionen Franken täglich gaben er und sein Gefolge bei ihrem Besuch in Genf aus. Das reicht für mehr als den nackten Lebensunterhalt. Schierer Luxus? Für Hoheit und Hofstaat nicht unbedingt; die Herrschaften sind sich diesen Lebensstil gewöhnt, gähnender Alltag für sie. Auch Luxus ist relativ. Und eine Frage der Perspektive.

Luxus ist Begierde ignorieren

Luxus ist das, was uns fehlt. Oder was wir nur knapp besitzen. Wir begehren, bitte schön, mehr davon. Wollen mal ganz hochgestochen zu den Sternen greifen und residieren im Burj Al Arab in Dubai, dem teuersten Hotel der Welt. Nur ein einziges Mal an dem nippen, was die Superreichen normalerweise unter sich auskosten. Allein diese Begierde verrät uns als Banausen. Karl Lagerfeld lehrt: "Wahrer Luxus ist, ihn einfach zu ignorieren. Aufhören, sich nach oben zu vergleichen." Lagerfelds Vorstellungen bewegen sich weg vom schnöden Mammon. Er hat höhere Visionen: "Luxus ist Freunde um sich haben, ein gutes Gespräch." Ins gleiche Horn stösst Donald Trump. Der New Yorker Immobilien-Gigant ist eben doch kein reiner Materialist: "Für mich ist Luxus meine Arbeit, meine Gesundheit und das Zusammensein mit einem Menschen, den ich liebe." Wer in materieller Hinsicht wunschlos glücklich ist, hat gut reden.

Luxus ist Niedergang und Dekadenz

An der Schnittstelle von politischer Macht, ökonomischer Potenz, ökologischen Bedenken und moralischen Prinzipien entfaltet der Luxus seine schillernde Wirkung. Weil es in seinem Wesen liegt, vom Mass abzuweichen, gilt er unter Moralaposteln als masslos. In der Tat wurde ausgelassene Prachtentfaltung manchen Hochkulturen zum Verhängnis: Luxus hat auch mit Dekadenz zu tun, mit Niedergang. Kommt Not, erwacht bekanntlich der Erfindergeist; unser unermüdliches Trachten nach Komfort und die ewige Lust am Luxus sind Antriebsräder im komplizierten System der Ökonomie. Sobald der Mensch Tech und High Tech austüftelt, befindet er sich wieder auf dem Weg nach oben – zum Leben in Saus und Braus.

Luxus ist der entscheidende Unterschied

Weder Kaschmirpulli noch Rolex können freilich die endgültigen Synonyme für Luxus sein. Solche Erkenntnis fiel Wallpaper-Gründer Tyler Brûlé wie Schuppen von den Augen, nachdem er als verwundeter Kriegsreporter im Spital erwachte – noch einmal davongekommen. Seit der Lifestyle-Experte ein zweites Leben, kostbare Zeit und seine geräumige Wohnung wider Erwarten zurück gewonnen hat, definiert er das Thema Luxus komplexer als zuvor: "Zeit und Platz" sind für das "gebrannte Kind" nun das Allerhöchste. Auch David Bosshart, Trendforscher und Leiter des Gottlieb-Duttweiler-Instituts in Rüschlikon (GDI), schätzt Zeit und Raum als wichtigste Luxus-Faktoren ein: "Heute beanspruchen tendenziell immer mehr Leute immer mehr Fläche. Wohlstand bedeutet mehr Raum." Das gilt für alle Lebenslagen – nicht nur fürs tägliche Wohnen. John Naisbitt, Urvater der Trendforschung und Autor des Bestsellers "Megatrends", gelangte zur selben Erkenntnis: "In einer Welt, wo alle die gleichen High Tech Produkte anbieten, ist High Touch der alles entscheidende Unterschied", schreibt er in seinem Buch "High Tech – High Touch".

Luxus ist Kürzertreten

Die Glaubwürdigkeit eines Produkts ist ausschlaggebend, das gilt auch für kostspielige Uhren und Schmuck – Symbole ersten Ranges für Luxus. Tiffany glänzt mit einer Spur Faszination mehr, seit Audrey Hepburn den New Yorker Juwelier im Film "Breakfast at Tiffany's" endgültig verklärte. Interessant also zu erfahren, was

John Loring, Design-Direktor des Nobelhauses, unter Luxus versteht. Der Dauer-Jet-Setter ist ebenfalls auf den Geschmack mit der Zeit gekommen. Luxus bedeutet für ihn, neben den üblichen Annehmlichkeiten, die das Leben komfortabler gestalten – wie Schönheit, Intelligenz und Charme – in allererster Linie Zeit. Leider ist Zeit nicht käuflich, und wieviel uns davon im Leben noch bleibt, wissen wir nicht. Nach Kürzertreten anstatt Karriere sehnt sich der moderne Mensch: Als "Downshifting-Trend" definiert der deutsche Zukunftsforscher Matthias Horx dieses neue Streben nach Lebensqualität. Nicht mehr der Konsum von Ware, die dank dem Marketing-Zaubertrick "Verknappung" zum raren Luxusgut stilisiert wird, macht uns glücklich. Matthias Horx stellt fest, dass wir immer mehr Geld ausgeben für Dienstleistungen und immer weniger für Dinge. Dienstbare Geister, die uns mehr Freizeit garantieren, sind der neue Luxus, die Putzfrau die echte Perle.

Luxus ist menschlich, allzumenschlich

Zukunftspotential wittert David Bosshart auch im Sektor Schönheit: "Es geht nicht mehr darum, den Menschen von irgendwelchen Defekten zu befreien, sondern ihn perfekter zu machen als er von Natur aus ist." Unverwüstliche Schönheit wäre geradezu das Nonplusultra an Luxus. So solid wie das Handwerkliche, das sich neuerdings grosser Hochschätzung erfreut. Authentische Einzelstücke sind gesuchte Objekte mit Symbolwert, dank der persönlichen Geschichte, die sie erzählen. "Heute hat Handgenähtes den Stellenwert von Luxus", doziert Yohji Yamamoto. "Weil nichts so teuer ist wie die menschliche Arbeitskraft." Die schlägt sich denn auch handfest auf den Preis einer handgefertigten Kelly-Bag von Hermès nieder oder einer Tasche von Louis Vuitton, die aussieht, als hätte ihre Besitzerin sie eigenhändig mit Graffiti besprayt. Meschliches, Allzumenschliches, behaupten Trend-Experten, mache der blanken Markenmanie ernsthaft Konkurrenz. Das Geschäft mit dem Luxus ist eine Gratwanderung, wie Louis Vuitton-Manager Jörg Zerbock zugibt: "Die Leute wollen schön angezogen sein, aber es muss mehr dahinter stecken, man kann sich nicht durchmogeln. Wir brauchen die Fähigkeit, immer wieder zu überraschen: fundiert, kein Strohfeuer", versucht er das Unbegreifliche zu erklären.

Luxus ist Ballast über Bord werfen

Luxus, darin sind sich die Gurus unter den Trendpropheten einig, wird in Zukunft mehr sein als eine Tasche im feinen Tragsack. Er wird zunehmend immaterielle Züge annehmen, kann infolgedessen Wissen bedeuten; mehr Ruhe vielleicht, seinen Rhythmus leben, sich von Ballast befreien. Klammern wir uns nicht krampfhaft an Güter, die wir für Zeiten horten, in denen wir dereinst mehr Musse haben werden. Denn ungewiss ist, ob unsere physischen Voraussetzungen dann noch intakt sind für alles, was wir uns ausgemalt und vorgenommen haben. Gesundheit wird dannzumal wahrscheinlich der wahre Luxus sein und vielleicht der letzte, der uns bleibt. Augen, die lesen und sehen. Ohren, die hören. Füsse, die gehen können. Und ein Hirn, das funktioniert. Einigermassen. Oder gar so differenziert, dass es den echten Luxus im Leben erkennt. Gerade noch rechtzeitig. /////

Margrit Gaudard
1940 geboren in Bern, phil I Studium an den Universitäten Bern und Neuenburg; Public Relations für Luxusmarken wie Armani, Helena Rubinstein, Lanvin, Ralph Lauren; Redakteurin bei Harper's Bazaar; nun schreibt sie seit Jahren als freie Journalistin regelmässig für eine Reihe von Wohn- und Lifestylezeitschriften (Lounge, L'Eveil Culturel, Magazin BaZ, Schöner Wohnen Schweiz) sowie für Zeitungen, namentlich für die Basler Zeitung und Der Landbote in Winterthur.

M LOVES SCRABBLE

SCRABBLE
DELUXE

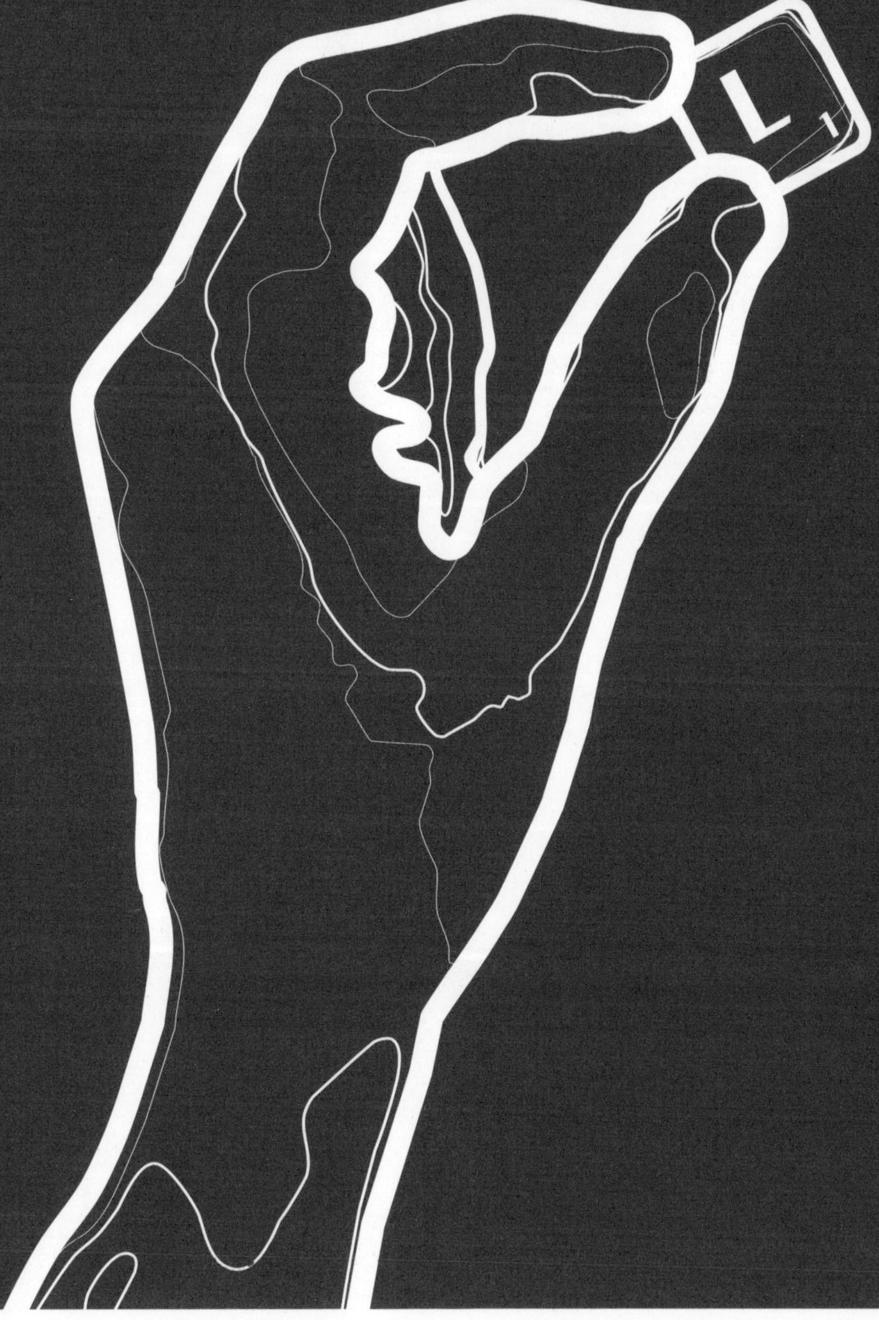

M
PONY
QUALITY
HENNESSY
PLATIN
BILLS
INDIVIDUALITY
FASHION
ROSES
FERRARI
JETSET
CHILD
ROLEX
BUTLER
LUXURY
MOON
OXYGEN
SUN
VERTU
ARMANI
LUCKY
TAXATION
MILLION
MOTHER
CENTENARY
TRUE
DOLLAR
CUISINE
ETERNITY
GOLD
FAMILY
SPECIMEN
DIAMOND
HYATT
CHILL
ONASSIS
POSH
ENVY
BURBERRY
KINGDOM
NICE
DELUXE
POMPOUS
FREEDOM
MAYBACH
MONACO
CONCORDE
NATURE
HEALTH
ROYAL
TIFFANY
CHEF
DOWJONES
RICH
GEM

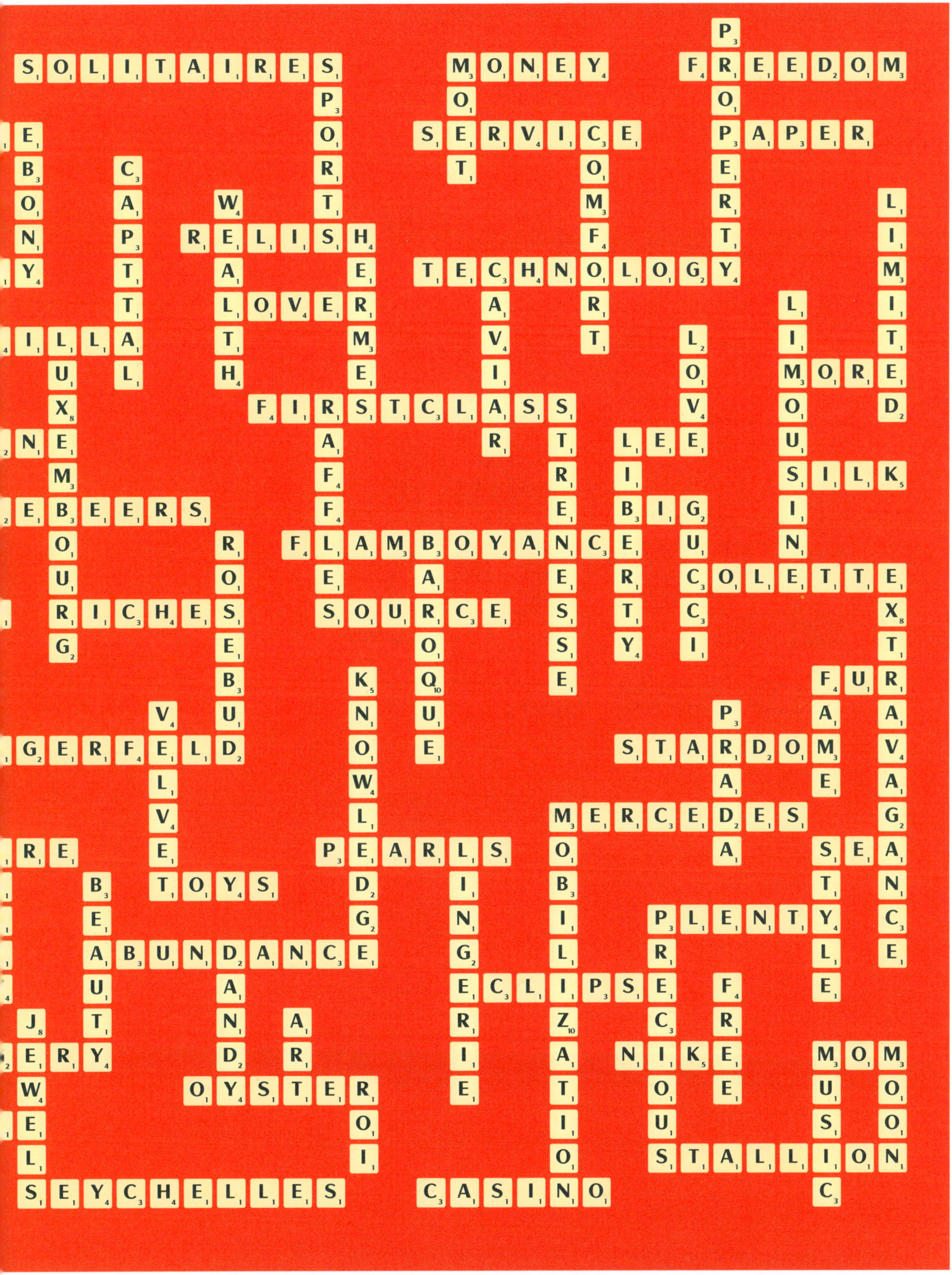
SOLITAIRES
MONEY
FREEDOM
SERVICE
PAPER
RELISH
TECHNOLOGY
LOVER
ILLA
MORE
FIRSTCLASS
NE
LEE
SILK
EBEERS
BIG
FLAMBOYANCE
COLETTE
RICHES
SOURCE
FUR
GERFELD
STARDOM
MERCEDES
RE
PEARLS
SEA
TOYS
PLENTY
ABUNDANCE
ECLIPSE
ERY
NIKE
MOM
OYSTER
STALLION
SEYCHELLES
CASINO
PROPERTY
SPORTS
MOST
COMFORT
EBONY
CAPITAL
WEALTH
HERMES
LIMITED
CAVIAR
LOVE
LIMOUSIN
LUXEMBOURG
STRENESSE
LIBERTY
GUCCI
RAFFLES
ROSEBUD
BAROQUE
EXTRAVAGANCE
KNOWLEDGE
VELVET
FAME
PRADA
STYLE
MOBILIZATION
LINGERIE
BEAUTY
PRECIOUS
FREE
MUSIC
MOON
SAND
ART
ROI
JEWEL

DENKAUFGABE

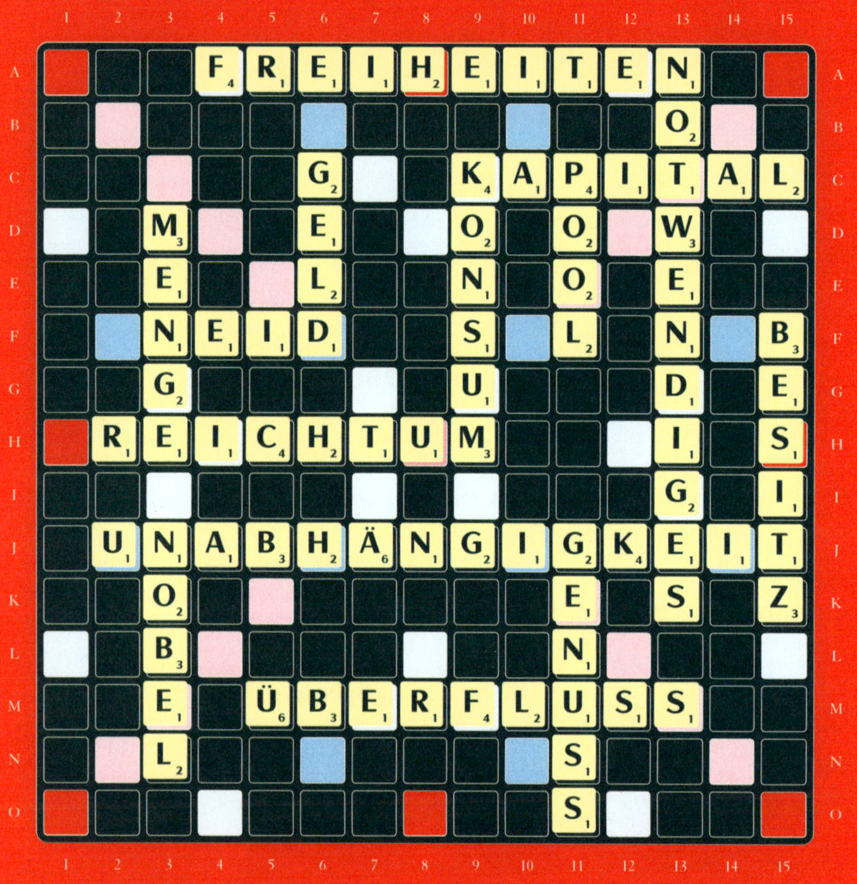

ÖMPPO

Dreifacher Wortwert

Doppelter Wortwert

Dreifacher Buchstabenwert

Doppelter Buchstabenwert

Für Scrabble Nichtkenner: Scrabble ist ein Buchstabenspiel, an dem sich zwei, drei oder vier Spieler beteiligen können. Aufgabe des Spielers ist es, aus Buchstabensteinen mit unterschiedlichem Wert Wörter zusammenzusetzen und so auszulegen, dass sie nach Art eines Kreuzworträtsels miteinander in Verbindung stehen. Siehe oben.

Mit der richtigen Positionierung der Buchstabensteine Ö, M, P, P, O lassen sich 66 Punkte erzielen. Lösungswort und Stand-Koordinaten: WinScrabble@M-Publication.com

Play&Win. Wie lautet die Lösung? Scrabble Magnetics & Scrabble Deluxe.

WinScrabble@M-Publication.com. Einsendeschluss: 30.11.2003. Der Rechtsweg ist ausgeschlossen.

Geiz ist grässlich

Deutschland – kein schönes Land in dieser Zeit. Schlussverkauf wohin man blickt. Flächendeckend schlechte Stimmung auf allen Bildschirmen und in allen Kommentarspalten. Wir müssen sparen, sparen, sparen, lautet die Parole. Nicht Nachrichten, sondern Sonderangebote stellen die wichtigsten Schlagzeilen des Jahres.

Das Lamento titelt ein genialer Claim, der, vorgesehen eigentlich zur Profilierung eines Handelsunternehmens, mutiert ist zur zentralen Programmatik des Zeitgeistes: "Geiz ist geil": wer billig einkauft, der ist klüger, wer im Alltag auf Einkaufsvergnügen verzichtet, der handelt vorbildlich. Selten war eine Werbeparole verantwortungsloser für die Volkswirtschaft und schädlicher für das Gemeinwohl. Und noch nie war ein Claim freudloser, genussfeindlicher. Denn wir leben nicht, um zu arbeiten, sondern wir arbeiten, um zu leben. Wer sich dem eigenen Genuss verwehrt, der verweigert sich der Lebensfreude. Wer spart, hat mutmaßlich mehr auf dem Konto, dafür sicher weniger an Lebensqualität.

"Geil" ist etwas anderes – Geiz ist nur mehr grässlich

Ist derjenige clever zu nennen, der mit steifem Rückrat an den Schaufenstern vorbei wandert, ohne einen Blick zu verschwenden? Ist derjenige zu bewundern, der seinen Kleinwagen ein Jahr weiter fährt, obwohl er sich seit Jahren ein Cabrio wünscht? Eben.

Wir haben uns – leider ziemlich deutsch – in eine Dauerdepression geflüchtet. Konsumverweigerung nützt niemandem. Der Volkswirtschaft nicht – denn ohne Absatz geht es nicht voran. Dem Konsumenten nicht, denn sein Arbeitsplatz bleibt unsicher und er verliert an Lebensqualität.

Es geht mir nicht darum, einer wilden Verschwendungssucht das Wort zu reden oder zum sinnlosen Prassen aufzufordern. Aber wir müssen uns selbst entfesseln. Wir müssen uns wieder jenen kleinen Genuss erlauben, der das Leben lebenswert macht. Nur wer genießt, kann auch konsumieren. Wir wollen nicht alle Brioni-Anzüge tragen, aber wir wollen uns freuen können, wenn wir einem Brioniträger begegnen. Wir wollen nicht immer und jede Stunde Zigarren rauchen, aber wir wissen um deren Genuss und stecken uns ab und zu eine an. Derzeit erleben wir nur das Gegenteil: Die bundesdeutsche Neidgesellschaft treibt sich mit ihrem Sparzwang die Konsum- und mit dieser auch die Lebensfreude aus.

Das ist sogar sozial nivellierend. Peter Sloterdijk grübelte kürzlich über "geringfügigen Haushaltsschwankungen", die mit einer "kollektiven Panik vor Verarmung" beantwortet würden. Das sei "demokratiefeindlich": denn die Demokratisierung des Luxus zu Beginn des 20. Jahrhunderts sei das größte Experiment der modernen Gesellschaft. Anders gewendet: Wer heute auf zuviel verzichtet, der senkt seinen Sozialstatus. Wer nicht mehr konsumiert, der unterscheidet sich nicht mehr. Denn nur im Konsum und in der Ausprägung der eigenen Lebensart liegt die Chance, sich ein wenig von seiner Umgebung abzusetzen, anderen Individualität vorzuleben.

Fast möchte man meinen, das neue gesamte Deutschland taumelt in den grauen langweiligen Alltag der versunkenen DDR zurück. Was für eine grässliche Vorstellung. Umso ärgerlicher, dass kaum jemand seine Stimmung pro Genuss, pro Luxus, pro Lebensart erhebt. Kein Plädoyer im Feuilleton, das freudvoll an erlebnisreiche Nächte in Berlin erinnert. Keine Generation Golf, die unverfangen genussfreudig im Metropolitan Richtung Nordsee braust. Nur Erbsenzähler, die mit der Bundesbahn um den Preis der Bahncard hadern oder dicht an dicht die Sitzreihen der Billig-Airlines füllen.

Wirtschaft und Politik setzen vielmehr noch eins drauf, wenn es darum geht, die allgemeine Spardepression zu fördern. Graugesichtige Bedenkenträger, kreativ nur in der Erfindung neuer Steuervorschläge, sprechen ständig neue Mahnungen aus, bitte an Verantwortung gegenüber dieser und jener Allgemeinheit zu denken. Um im gleichen Gegenzug das fehlende jeglichen Konsumklimas wehleidig zu beklagen. Sie sollten es besser wissen.

Luxus ist mehr als nur eine Sonderausgabe der WirtschaftsWoche: Es ist ein Manifest. Gegen Schnäppchenmentalität, gegen Untergangs-Propheten, gegen Geiz-Asketen und all diejenigen, welche die Trümmernostalgie des Nachkriegsdeutschlands noch heute als die beste aller Lebensarten empfinden. Der Spruch "Geiz ist geil" ist lebensfeindlich. Er mag seinem Absender nützen, uns allen vergällt er nur den Spaß am Leben. Es sei daran erinnert: Wir haben nur dieses eine. /////

Dr. Andreas Knaut
Jahrgang 1960. Leiter des Bereiches Unternehmenskommunikation der Verlagsgruppe Handelsblatt GmbH.

M empfiehlt
Wer von Luxus nicht genug hat, darf sich auf die "WirtschaftsWoche Luxus" freuen. Erscheinungsdatum: 30. Oktober 2003

⇛ www.handelsblatt.de

PHOTOGRAPHY BY
KIMBERLY LLOYD

DOV CHARNEY.
JUNE 2003 – ROOM 231
HILTON FRANKFURT.

BY KIMBERLY LLOYD

False tribalism – the hallmark of contemporary luxury

Dov Charney's view on the apparel industry, false tribalism and his way of redefining the American dream.

A simple piece of clothing, a T-shirt, and it is blank. What is so revolutionary about your T-shirts? Is it the quality of the T-shirts, the different styles or the manufacturing process, your lean management, your politics or the strong social system you have built for a "sweatshop-free" community?
_The strategy is to make T-shirts young people love to wear. By treating workers well and keeping the manufacturing vertically integrated with the design, administrative, logistical, and financial elements, we are able to optimise the quality. In order to create efficiency within the workplace, it becomes critical that there is low turnover and high worker morale – that is where the sweatshop-free idea comes in. So it is socialism, but only to support the capitalism of the company. To ensure the financial security of the company, our philosophy is to ensure that everyone touched by our business process has a positive experience, be they garment workers or customers.

How strong are Americans in the design business?
_Speaking only for the commodity apparel business, I think the Americans had a heritage of manufacturing commodity apparel, which became the icons of the hippy and boomer generation. Items like the 1970s versions of Levi's cords, Hanes underwear, or Champion sweatshirts are known worldwide and are still displayed at vintage stores all over the Western world.

Did European companies dictate the pricing rules?
_As Americans tried to adopt the collections approach from Europe, this heritage got lost. European jeans makers were getting $120 for their jeans, and the Americans were only getting $25, so they tried to emulate the collections approach and I think they fucked up the American system where styles would not change for long periods of time, like Levi's 501s, etc. Furthermore, as the boomers got older, these companies lost their connection to youth, and they got hyper-concerned with moving offshore, which deflated the price of the garments, but distracted the majors from reconnecting to the next generation. They lost their touch. Had they focused on optimising their products and not chasing cheap labour, their companies would have been in better shape.

Where does American design come from?
_On the fashion side, right now I think some of the most interesting design work comes out of Los Angeles, but I may be biased.

Why do you consider America as your final destination – productionwise?
_We are not American nationalists and we think our business model can be taken to any region of the world. But we will always pay the US dollar minimum wage set by the federal government. If we open a factory in China, we will sell our T-shirts in China, and we will pay at least the US dollar minimum wage of $5.15 per hour. It is a new US imperialism. We will not charge US dollar prices, but pay poverty wages, because we are too good for that. We are too smart to steal. We are next-generation capitalists and to pay shit wages would be to confirm that our self-righteousness is full of shit.

Which brands do you consider intact in their value for the consumer, their corporate communication and their company politics?
_Sorry, but I can't think of one right now.

Is branding a garment an act of "artificially" claiming it as a luxurious product?
_Branding is often a form of false tribalism. We want to sell our garments based on our product. We don't want people buying our product because of the brand image, but because they love our products.

You cannot tolerate labels on your personal clothing. Why not?
_Because it represents false tribalism. For the same reason I don't believe in God. »

Being "maverick of the morning" on CNN is hard work, but you still find plenty of time to see employees. Health insurance, dental care, free on-site massages, English classes... You are striving to pioneer a political movement of human rights – pure altruism?
_American Apparel is not altruism. It is capitalism. We treat our workers well to advance our business, to create an environment of efficiency, where everyone wins.

Madonna's latest album is about "The American Dream" and you speak of "The Redesign of the American Dream" – you condemn moneymaking as the only purpose of a company.
_I do not believe in America as a country any more. I believe in America as a value system, which symbolises for me freedom. This can be traced back to England and further back to Greece. Life, liberty, property, pursuit of happiness, or as the French put it, "liberté, fraternité, égalité ...". This is what America is all about. But the border system is over. Religion is over. Tribalism is over. I believe that people should be able to move freely worldwide. To move or migrate where they want. That everyone has these inalienable rights. That everyone, as stated in the Magna Carta of 1215, can sell his labour in England. When the world is open and people can move freely, the divide between the rich and poor will decease and Adam Smith's invisible hand will play a role of natural equalisation. Open borders are possible ... look at Europe, for example. So my American dream is that everyone can feel protected by the US Bill of Rights worldwide, not just US citizens on US soil.

The union's the biggest enemy of the labour market. Are they to be tolerated?
_I firmly believe in collective bargaining rights. I would never frustrate a union effort by my workers. But I also think that people cannot fault "American Apparel" if our workers have not sought a union. For us to have imposed a union would have been a false move. Unions have also become a form of branding and false tribalism. Unions can be critical in helping improve working conditions, but they are not always the answer, and the concept often relies on the idea that unions are going to fight honestly for the worker against bad employers. But not all unions are good and not all employers are bad. Many sweatshops are unionised. Furthermore, the union concept implies that workers and management do not have common goals, whereas at "American Apparel" we see the welfare of our workers as being critical to our company's success.

What does the term luxury mean to you?
_Luxury for me personally would mean perfect functionality and efficiency. Luxury is the perfect use of resources whereby no one in the community – be they customers, suppliers, the environment or shareholders – is getting damaged by the process of production. That is how I see it. But for contemporary society right now, I think luxury is false and dishonest. It is backed up by false tribalism whereby there is no real substance. It is often based on manufactured hype. Like the diamond industry. The scarcity of diamonds is completely fabricated by the De Beers family. Yet underneath the surface, people are getting severely exploited to support the diamond industry. The coupling of false hype and exploitation seems to have become the hallmark of contemporary luxury.

Is luxury a matter of the price tag?
_The luxury market is marked by high margins and high failure rates, which render the concept of contemporary luxury. /////

Dov Charney
Dov Charney, born on 31 January 1969 in Montreal, is the founder and senior partner of American Apparel. Charney started his entrepreneurship aged 11 by launching a newspaper. Today, he is America's third largest T-shirt manufacturer after Hanes and Fruit of the Loom.

⇒ American Apparel
747 Warehouse St., Los Angeles CA 90021, USA
T. +1.213.488.0226, www.americanapparel.net

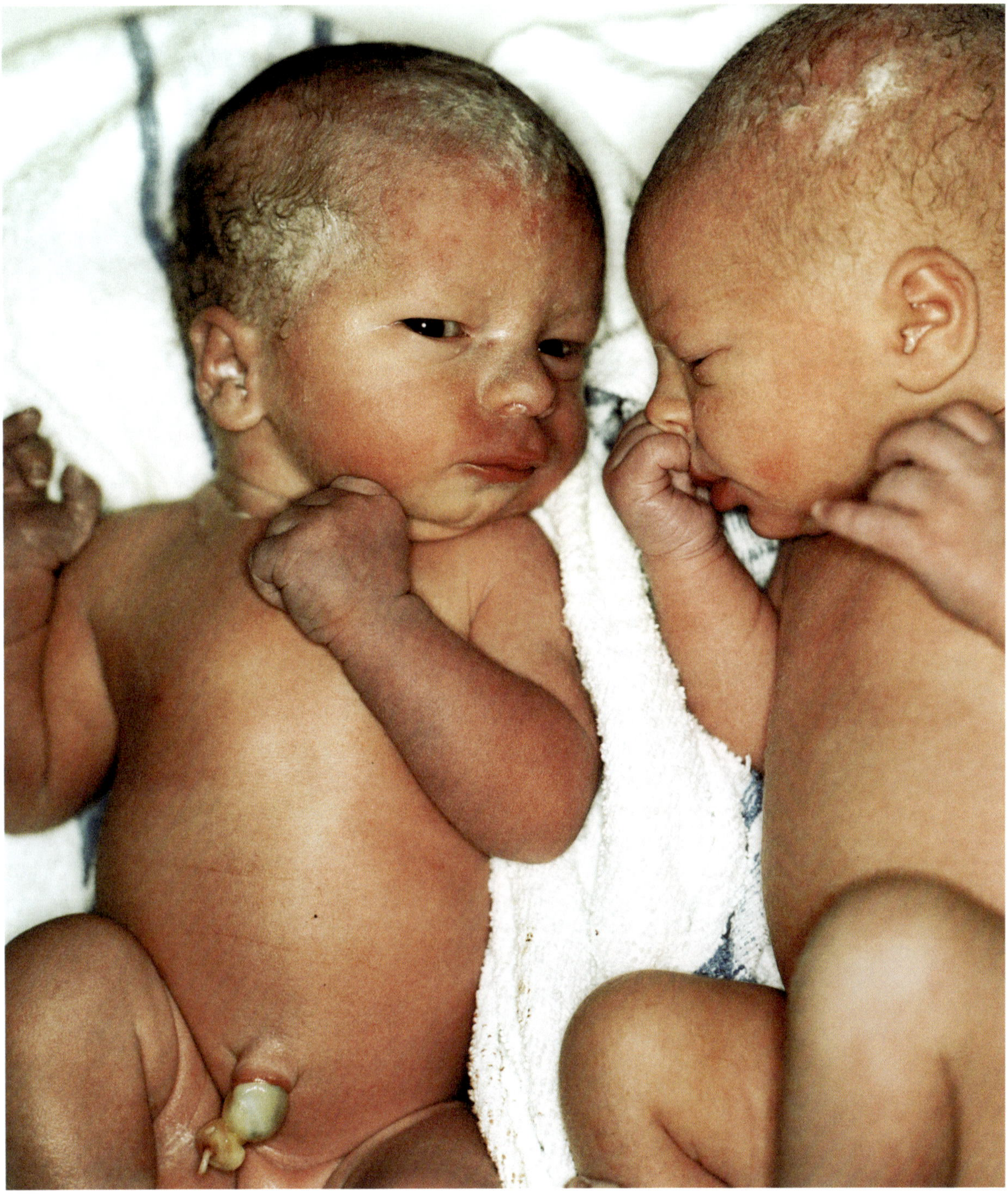

Du lebst mono.

PHOTOGRAPHY BY
SUSANNE WALSTRÖM

WORDS BY
PIERO BORSELLINO

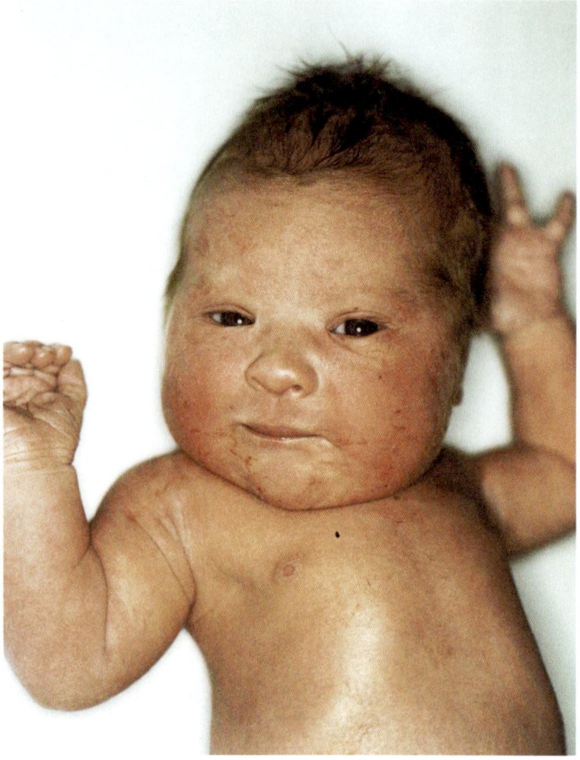
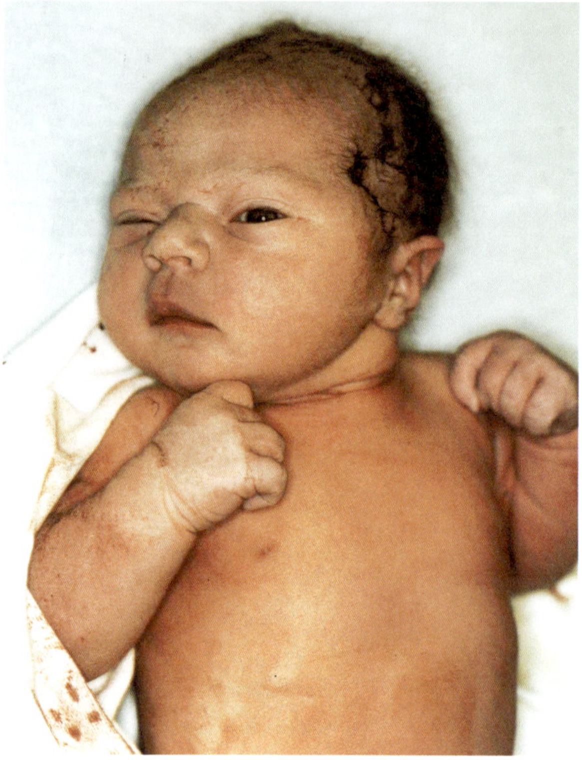

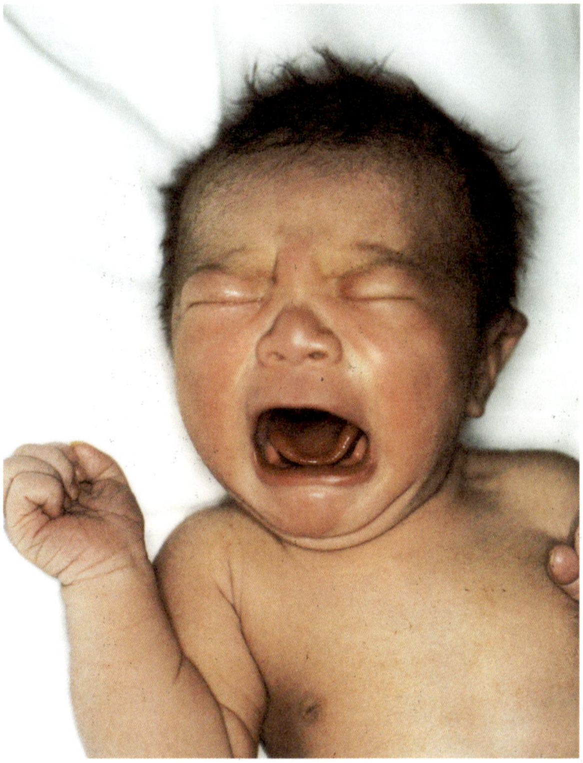 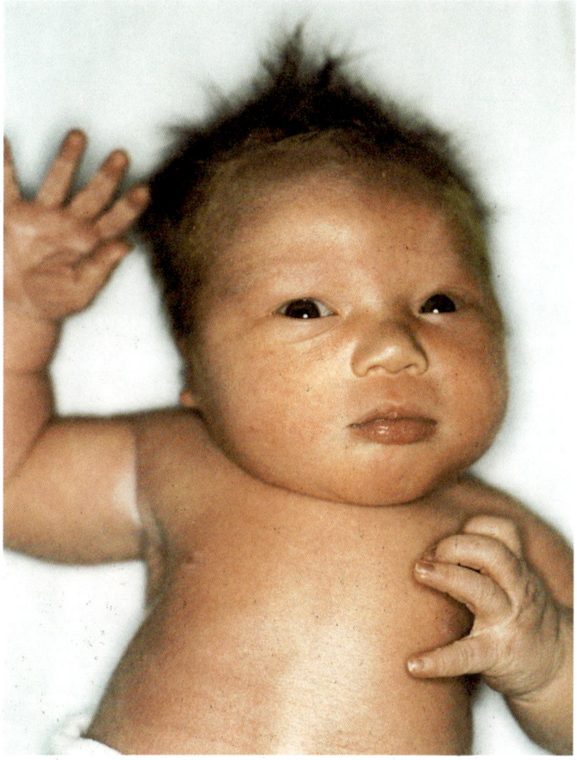

Das Leben gibt es nicht im Doppelpack.
Nicht auf Knopfdruck, playstation-like,
in unzähliger Menge. Und auch nicht
als hinduistischen Reinkarnations-Loop.
Jedenfalls nicht nachweislich.

Fest steht: Du hast nur ein Leben.
Einen Geburtstermin. Und eine einzige Deadline,
die nicht in deinem Timer steht.

Lebe daher deine eigene Religion: Denke stereo.

PHOTOGRAPHY BY
LYN BALZER & ANTHONY PERKINS

Viagra für den Artenschutz

Was hat ein Sack Reis in China mit dem Weltklima zu tun? Verblüffend viel. Weil das Wasser knapp wurde, hörten chinesische Reisbauern damit auf, ihre Felder ständig zu fluten, sondern ließen sie zwischendurch trocken fallen. Ohne Feuchtigkeit können Methan produzierende Bodenbakterien nicht leben. Folglich sank die Methanemission in Ostasien. Methan ist ein Treibhausgas, das zur Klimaerwärmung beiträgt. Chinas Bauern haben also, ohne es zu wollen oder überhaupt nur daran zu denken, einen erheblichen Beitrag zum Klimaschutz geleistet.

Egal ob an der Börse, in der Politik oder im Umweltschutz. Kaum haben Experten ihre Prognosen aufgestellt, Trends verkündet und Pläne entwickelt, um in die Zukunft zu steuern. Da schmeißt eine unvorhergesehene Nebenwirkung alles um. "Ja, mach nur einen Plan. Sei nur ein großes Licht. Und mach dann noch 'nen zweiten Plan. Gehn tun sie beide nicht", dichtete Brecht. Obwohl Ökologie die Wissenschaft vom oftmals überraschenden Wechselspiel der verschiedenen Lebewesen ist, sträuben sich viele Umweltschützer, Nebenwirkungen wahrzunehmen. Womöglich liegt das daran, dass sie einem zutiefst konservativen Weltbild nachhängen. Naturschutz heißt auf Englisch "Conservation", Bewahrung. Viele Umweltschützer möchten den heutigen Zustand der Welt in alle Zukunft bewahren oder die vermeintlich gute alte Zeit zurückholen. Veränderungen können sie sich nur als Desaster vorstellen: Das Klima kippt, der Wald stirbt, die Bevölkerungsexplosion frisst den Planeten. Kann es nicht auch mal andersrum sein? Gibt es niemals Kippeffekte zum Guten?

Die Natur ist nicht statisch. Sie war ein paar Millionen Jahre im Fitnessstudio. Evolution bedeutet unaufhörlichen Wandel, Werden und Vergehen. Und dieser Wandel kann ganz anders ausfallen, als es in den Beschlüssen der deutschen Umweltverbände steht. Wer hätte zum Beispiel gedacht, dass die meisten Vogelarten in Deutschland nicht in Naturschutzgebieten leben, sondern in Großstädten? In Berlin ist die Artenvielfalt viel größer als im Nationalpark Bayerischer Wald.

Die Vergangenheit ist voller Beispiele für solche verblüffenden Nebeneffekte, mit denen niemand je gerechnet hatte. Die im 18. Jahrhundert bis auf klägliche Reste gerodeten Wälder Europas dehnten sich wieder aus, als die Dampfmaschine die Förderung von Kohle aus großer Tiefe möglich werden ließ. Kohle ersetzte das Heizen mit Holz. Der Wald erholte sich.

Dass seit Anfang des 20. Jahrhunderts Deutschland, die USA und die meisten anderen Nationen den Walfang aufgaben, lag nicht daran, dass sie plötzlich ihr Herz für Wale entdeckten. Sie brauchten das Walöl schlicht und einfach nicht mehr, weil inzwischen das Erdöl entdeckt worden war.

Einer der wichtigsten Umwelttrends der letzten zwei Jahrzehnte ist die so genannte Effizienzrevolution: Die Wirtschaft in den Industrieländern benötigt um zu wachsen immer weniger Rohstoffe und Energie. Dies ist keinem Umweltprogramm, sondern dem Computer zu verdanken, der die Effizienz vieler Produktionsprozesse drastisch erhöhte.

Die eindringlichste Ikone der weltweiten Ökobewegung ist das Foto vom blauen Planeten im schwarzen All. Es wurde millionenfach gedruckt, prangt auf Buchtiteln, CD-Covers und Postern. Doch es ist nichts weiter als ein Nebenprodukt der Raumfahrt. Niemand bei der NASA hatte damals Umweltschutz im Sinn.

In Ostasien änderten sich unterdessen nicht nur die Reisanbaumethoden. Auch der Artenschutz erhielt überraschende Hilfe. Seit dem Siegeszug von Viagra hat die Nachfrage für obskure Naturarzneien aus Tiger, Nashorn und anderen Tieren erheblich nachgelassen. Blaue Pillen schützen seltene Arten, trockener Reis verändert das Klima – natürlich kann man auf solche unerwartbaren Nebenwirkungen nicht bauen. Es ist jedoch genauso falsch, sie zu ignorieren. /////

Michael Miersch
Geboren 1956 in Frankfurt am Main, volontierte bei der "taz" und war Redakteur der Umweltmagazine "Chancen" und "Natur". Seit 1993 schreibt er als selbständiger Publizist für große Zeitungen, Zeitschriften und Radiosender im deutschsprachigen Raum. Darüber hinaus ist Miersch Autor zahlreicher Sachbücher und Dokumentarfilme, wofür er zahlreiche Auszeichnungen in den USA und Deutschland erhalten hat.

- Die Zukunft und ihre Feinde, Maxeiner/Miersch, Eichborn
  Das Mephisto-Prinzip, Maxeiner/Miersch, Eichborn
  Lexikon der Öko-Irrtümer, Maxeiner/Miersch, Eichborn
- www.maxeiner-miersch.de
  www.eichborn.de
- Siehe auch das Interview auf Seite 109. Die Mythenkiller: Michael Miersch und Dirk Maxeiner über Legenden und Lügen bezüglich Globalisierung, Branding und Kulturimperialismus.

Arab stallion "Amir" for sale

Bred by the Cheval Equine Foundation, this beautiful 1988 black stallion exemplifies the finest in Arabic breeding. He is sired by Sultan, one of the most influential sires of the post-war era. Sultan left an incomparable legacy in Poland and the United States through his highly prized daughters and sons. At the Cheval Equine Foundation you will find an ultimate collection of the world's most unique breeds – a combination of exceptional beauty, substance and outstanding athleticism. Amir's gentle nature and tractable temperament are hallmarks of the Sultan dynasty. For more information on his selected semen and family chronicle.
Cheval Equine Foundation: +1 (0)512 6345 89012

www.worldofhorses.co.uk
www.horses.co.uk
www.habitatforhorses.org
www.horses-and-horse-information.com
www.equineworld.net
www.horsehusbands.com

white asphalt
black asphalt
Dior

We cannot afford to do without luxuries

PHOTOGRAPHY BY
ANDREAS JOHANSSON _LUNDLUND.COM

FICTIONAL STORY BY
KRATHYN WHITE

STYLIST _LARS-FREDRIK SVEDBERG _LUNDLUND.COM
HAIR _CARINA FINNSTRÖM _MIKAS.SE
MAKE UP BY MAGDALENA ERIXON
FOR LANCÔME _MIKAS.SE
MODELS _STOCKHOLMSGRUPPEN
OSCAR, EMIL P, THOR
AND KARIN, LINNEA, ELIN AT _MIKAS.SE

EMIL WEARS
T-SHIRT WITH 3/4 LENGTH SLEEVES RAF SIMONSWHITE JEANS _HELMUT LANG. LACK BELT WITH METALLIC BUCKLE _MARTIN MARGIELA. STRING BELT WITH LEATHER ACCESSOIRES _DRIES VAN NOTEN. BLACK AND WHITE KEYRINGS _MARTIN MARGIELA. BLACK MINI-ARMBAG _RAF SIMONS. GLOVE _AGENT ANONYM AMSTERDAM. LOGO KEY-CHAIN _DIOR. VINTAGE MILITARY BOOTS CUSTOMISED BY _LARS-FREDRIK SVEDBERG.

Dear Keryl,

You won't believe it!

I found some of the most intense photographs that help explain the script idea we discussed last weekend – the idea about a trio of murderous dandies living together ménage à trois-style.

And the pictures totally play up to the idea of luxury we were discussing as one of the themes in the story. The boys in these pictures look totally detached ... like they're up to their eyeballs in designer ennui replete with token glamour puss fag hags.

I actually stole the pictures from this photographer I know, but that's another long and boring story, which can only be told after we've consumed large amounts of alcohol together.

I've put down some thoughts – the first ones that came to mind – based on immediate reactions to the pictures. It might prove helpful when we meet again to develop the script and storyboards because I lost the napkin from that restaurant where we started talking about this idea last week.

Anyways, I have to dash. It's starting to rain, my jeans are still on the line and I've got to get ready for Daniel's party, and this one promises to be interesting – it'll be the first time seven of his former ex-boyfriends will be in the same place at the same time. Rest assured I'm taking the camera and I'm also taking no prisoners!

Let me know what you think and I'll talk to you when you get back from France.

Krathyn

EMIL WEARS
VEST _ANN DEMEULEMEESTER.
TROUSERS _STRENESSE
VINTAGE LOOSE COLLAR
WITH KEYRING _MARTIN MARGIELA
HAT _JAQUES LE CORRE PARIS
BOOTS AS BEFORE
KARIN WEARS
OUTFIT BY _EMPORIO ARMANI

UPCOMING PAGES
THOR WEARS
BLACK&WHITE T-SHIRT BY _MARTIN MARGIELA.
LEATHER VEST _ANETTE OLIVIERI, LE SHOP STOCKHOLM
RIDING GLOVES AND TROUSERS STYLISTS OWN
BELT _MARTIN MARGIELA
PLASTIC BRACELET _HELMUT LANG
LEATHER KEY-CHAIN _PRADA
LEATHER BOOTS AS BEFORE
ELIN AND LINNEA BOTH WEAR
SKIRT, TOP AND SHOES _EMPORIO ARMANI

FILM SCRIPT

Soaked in luxury and stained with deception

Florian, Janosh and Andreas are friends and lovers, bored and beautiful, and obsessed with the idea of life as nothing more than a means to pursue luxury at any cost. While they appreciate all things artistic, they're more concerned with the latest YSL pants and the newest scent from Alexander McQueen, those jeans from Strenesse of a bag from Dior.

They are the modern dandies, albeit murderous ones: Darius, Maximillian and Vincent.

Their existence is justified by the pursuit of pure luxury. Young and without noble lineage, apart from the benefit of nouveau riche parents, they dedicate most of their time to social activities, especially the need to be seen at the right time, in the right place with the right people (usually themselves) and, most importantly, wearing the right things.

Their coolness is completely calculated and refined – obviously the result of hours spent looking at magazines and sitting in front of mirrors. I actually found a great quote from Baudelaire that helps frame their collective mindset: "A dandy does not do anything".

Our trio are elegant social rebels who sit around in this constant state of ennui, bitching about people and plotting to kill people they hate, who get in their way for some reason, make foolish fashion or other faux pas.

I think having the trio exist in a sexual sense would also add to the excitement and confusion, but the focus shouldn't be on their sexuality. While our trio can certainly be homosexual, it should be their breakthroughs in fashionable style which set them over and above anyone else they know. That and the fact they kill people.

This way of portraying them could be funny and obviously have something to do with their ultimate demise, whatever that may be.

Have you had any ideas about how to resolve this vague notion of a story at all? I certainly haven't. It might take another bottle (or seven) of Scotch to figure that one out. Some parting quotes I found while reading about dandies:

"One should either be a work of art, or wear a work of art." *Oscar Wilde*

"A dandy is a clothes-wearing man, a man whose trade, office and existence consists in the wearing of the clothes ... wisely and well." *Thomas Carlyle*

And most importantly ...

"We cannot afford to do without luxuries."
Oscar Wilde /////

PHOTOGRAPHY BY
PIERO BORSELLINO

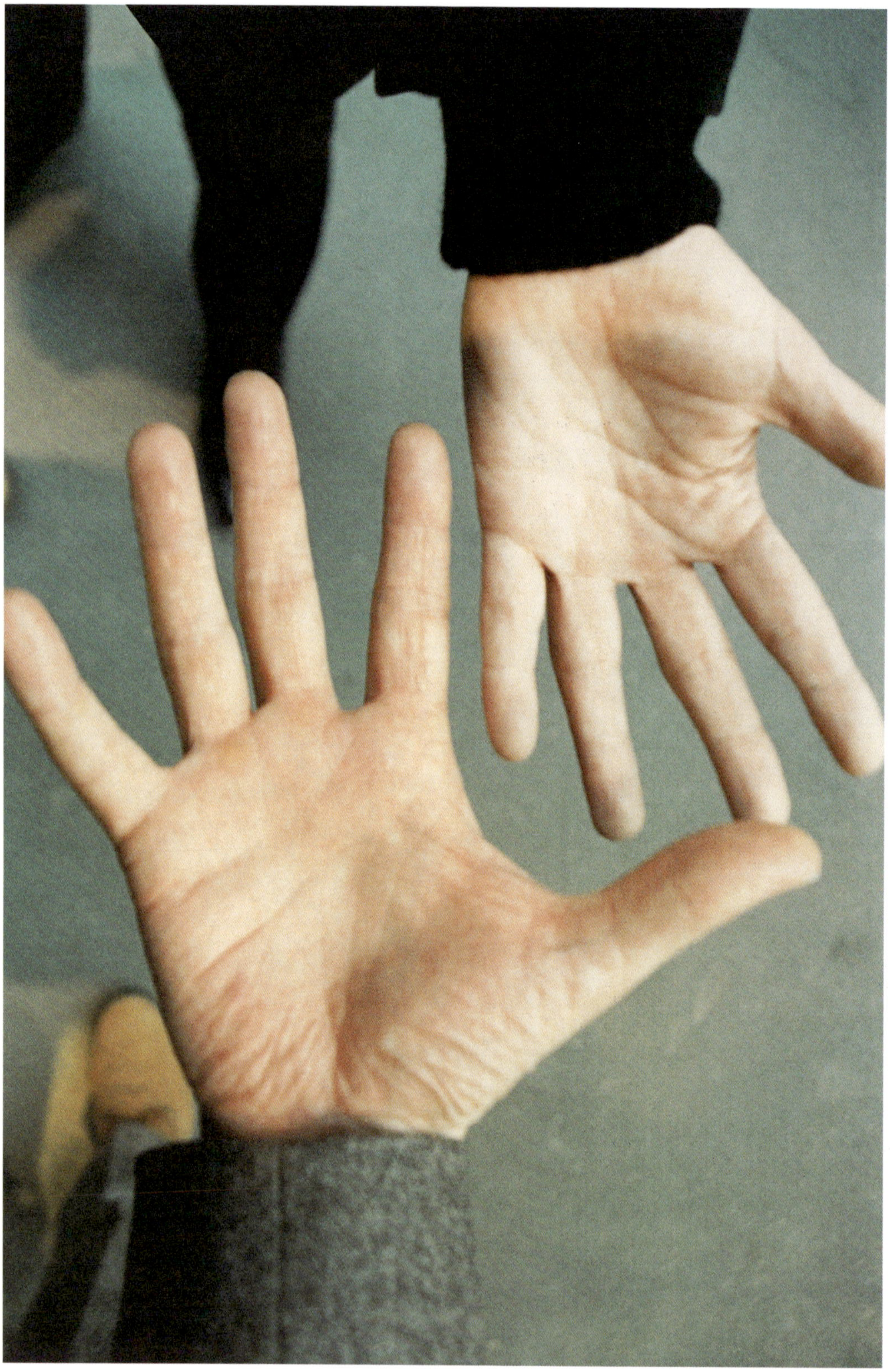

GABRIELE STREHLE & MATTEO THUN. APRIL 2003 – VIA MANZONI, MILANO.
PROCESSING LAB _FOTOQUICK-LABOR.DE

Wir brauchen nichts

Gabriele Strehle und Matteo Thun über Handwerkskunst, immaterielle Reichtümer und die Reduktion auf das Wesentliche.

Welche Bedeutung hat "Luxus" für Sie?
_Strehle: Luxus ist das Gegenteil von Glamour. Eine hausgemachte Pasta ist luxuriöser als Kaviar, denn die Dose kann ja jeder öffnen, aber etwas zu kochen, das ist eine andere Sache. Oder wenn ich auf meine Kindheit zurückschaue, dann erinnere ich mich an den Geruch der frischen Butter, frisch aus dem Butterfass, die nach Mandeln roch und aussah wie eine Creme. Mir ist das erst später bewusst geworden, dass das Luxus ist, da du das ja heute gar nicht mehr bekommst.

Ist "sich Luxus gönnen" gleichzusetzen mit "Reichtümer anhäufen" und übermäßigem Konsum von Luxusgütern?
_Thun: Es ist definitiv Luxus, weniger zu besitzen, Luxus ist die Beschränkung. Luxus ist Genuss der Subtraktion. Luxus ist, zu der Überzeugung zu kommen, dass wir nichts brauchen. Wir sollten vom Konsum Abstand nehmen und mit uns selbst ins Reine kommen. Wir leben in einer saturierten Gesellschaft und es ist fantastisch, zu bemerken, dass die Generation zwischen zehn und 15 sich heute von Konsum ganz eindeutig abwendet. Sie wendet sich nicht nur vom Konsum, sondern auch vom Branding ab. Produkte sollten funktional sein. Daher auch meine Sympathie für die Marke Strenesse. Es geht um Funktionalität, um das Wohlfühlen des Individuums und nicht um die Marke als Statussymbol, als Vorzeigeattribut.

_Strehle: Es ist vergangenheitsbezogen, Luxus mit Reichtum und Wohlstand zu vergleichen. Es muss nicht gleich das Teuerste oder ein Markenartikel sein. Luxus kann man in den banalsten Dingen finden – man sollte nur suchen können.
Die Zeit ist Luxus und für mich etwas ganz Wichtiges und Rares. Man ist gezwungen sich auf das Wesentliche im Leben zu konzentrieren, da man nicht Zeit für alles hat. In diesem Sinn gönne ich mir Luxus, wenn ich meine Tochter im einen Arm habe und meinen Mann auf der anderen Seite und einfach auf das Wasser schaue und diese Augenblicke genieße.

Frau Strehle, warum sollte eine Frau Ihre Kleidungsstücke tragen? Sehen Sie Ihr Mode-Label Strenesse als eine Luxusmarke?
_Strehle: Bei meiner Mode geht es nicht um eine Luxusmarke. Es geht um die Persönlichkeit der Frau und nicht darum, die Marke in den Vordergrund zu stellen. Es geht in erster Linie um die Akzeptanz der Persönlichkeit, so dass die Trägerin Zufriedenheit und Ausgeglichenheit ausstrahlt. Ich muss mich an die Frau erinnern und nicht an die Klamotten, nicht an das, was sie trägt. Das Wesentliche ist doch das Gesicht einer Frau, und wenn sie sich wohl fühlt in ihrer Kleidung, dann strahlt sie das den ganzen Tag aus. Und das wiederum macht mich in meiner Arbeit glücklich.

Viele Erfindungen zeichnen das 21. Jahrhundert aus, sei es das Internet, Handys oder andere "Commodities", die uns das Leben einfacher und luxuriöser gestalten lassen. Was glauben Sie, was für uns als Nächstes an besonderem Wert gewinnt?
_Strehle: Für mich ist es wichtig, dass die Tradition nicht verloren geht, da sie so viele wertvolle und lebenswichtige Informationen enthält. Wir sollten die Tradition wieder aufleben lassen und ihre Werte in unsere jetzige Zeit transportieren. Wenn du irgendeinen Beruf erlernt hast, vorzugsweise eine Handwerkskunst, dann hast du Tradition in dir, und das kannst du multiplizieren, übersetzen und transferieren. Matteo, hast du ein Handwerk erlernt?

_Thun: Ja, ich bin Keramiker. Meine Eltern haben mir als Kind nie Spielzeuge geschenkt. Mein Vater hat eine keramische Fabrik aufgebaut. Ich hatte die Möglichkeit, mir aus der Fabrik Tonstücke zu holen. Das nutzte ich, um mir mein Spielzeug selbst zu basteln. Ich töpferte Schildkröten – ein kleines Häufchen mit vier kleinen Extremitäten – und diese Schildkröten sind mein Kapital, auch heute noch. Ich weiß, dass ich mit meinen Fingern alles machen kann, was ich will, und ich habe mir als 4-Jähriger aus Mangel an Spielzeug selbst einen Zoo getöpfert. Dieser Zoo lebt heute auf andere Weise weiter.

Sind Kinder heutzutage etwas bequemer geworden?
_Thun: Leider muss ich heutzutage feststellen, dass nicht nur Erwachsene am Computer sitzen, sondern auch Kinder. Wenn ich meine Mitarbeiter am Computer beobachte – unheimlich schnell, wie sie am PC arbeiten – frage ich mich, ob das Gehirn dieses Tempo noch bewältigt und was die nächsten Jahre in dieser Hinsicht noch mit sich bringen.
Als Kreative leben wir mit einer wahnwitzigen Beschleunigung und mit dieser Problematik müssen wir uns zukünftig beschäftigen. Wir können alle Prozesse enorm beschleunigen, aber unser Gehirn besitzt ein bestimmtes Eigentempo, das sich nun mal nicht so erhöhen lässt, wie wir es wohl oft gerne hätten.

»

~~“Für mich ist es wichtig,~~
~~dass die Tradition~~
~~nicht verloren geht,~~

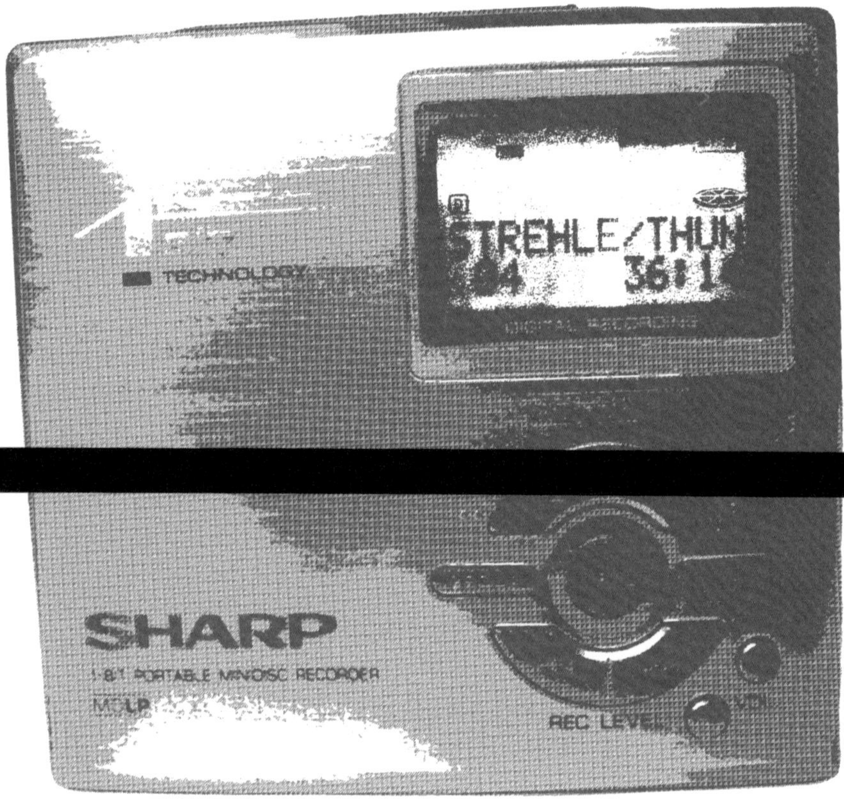

~~da sie so viele wertvolle~~
~~und lebenswichtige~~
~~Informationen enthält.”~~

Gabriele Strehle, Strenesse Chief Designer

Der Barock symbolisiert Luxus am treffendsten. Die damalige Mode, die Architektur, die Literatur und der Lebensstil waren stets opulent, prunkvoll und reich an Schmuckwerk. Ihre Designrichtung ist stets schlicht und spartanisch. Wie würden Sie Ihre Arbeit klassifizieren, vielleicht als "Minimalismus"?
_Strehle: Minimalismus heißt für mich Kälte, Statussymbole und Glamour. Minimalismus ist nach außen leben. Meine Arbeit bedeutet für mich, nach innen zu gehen, Wärme und Nähe zu suchen und kontinuierlich nach Möglichkeiten zu suchen, die Persönlichkeit der Frau erstrahlen zu lassen.

Zeigt sich das auch in der Kombination der Materialien?
_Strehle: Richtig. Matteo, zum Beispiel, kombiniert verschiedene Materialien wie Holz und Beton, die sich gegenseitig Wärme verleihen. In der Vergangenheit haben viele das kalte Alu verwendet und das unentwegt als Minimalismus bezeichnet.
Minimalismus in diesem Sinn gibt es für mich nicht – es ist eher die Reduktion auf das Wesentliche. Das ist mir ganz wichtig.

_Thun: Gabriele, das ist total wichtig, was du sagst. Das Gespräch könnte zu einem Missverständnis führen, nämlich, dass der überraschenderweise zur Jahrtausendwende abgelaufene Mainstream-Minimalismus gleichzusetzen wäre mit "less is a bore" – weniger ist Langeweile. Wir finden zurück zum klassischen Prinzip des Bauhauses, natürlich angereichert durch Stratifikationen von ca. 100 Jahren hin zu "less is more".
"Less is more" war im Bauhaus sehr funktional. Das war eine Zeit, in der man kämpfen musste. Es war eine schwierige Zeit und Kleidungsstücke waren primär dazu da, dass man nicht erfror, dass man sich schützte. Heute haben Kleider andere Funktionen bekommen und ich denke, diese emotionalisierende Komponente, die hinzugekommen ist, macht zwar die nächsten 20 Jahre so fantastisch spannend, aber eines ist klar, und das können wir beide sagen: Das hat nichts mit Minimalismus zu tun. Das ist eine andere Baustelle und das ist die Vergangenheit. Ich selbst war nie Minimalist und habe mich nie mit Minimalismus identifiziert. Meine Arbeit ist die Subtraktion von Überflüssigem und Reduktion auf das Wesentliche.

Sie legen beide sehr viel Wert auf die Materialien, die Sie für Ihre Arbeit verwenden, ob das den Bau des Designhotels Vigilius[1] oder die neue Menswear Collection von Strenesse betrifft. Im Bereich der Print-Publikationen wird oft glänzendes Papier, "Glossies", eingesetzt, um die Wertigkeit zu betonen. Worauf achten Sie beim Bücher- und Magazinkauf?
_Strehle: Ich brauche die Haptik. Ich achte auf die Struktur der Papiere, auf die Materialien, auf die Bindung und lege keinen großen Wert auf Glanz und Glamour. Es gibt in der Tat viele Glossies, die ich erst gar nicht anfasse. Beim mir ist das ganz stark ein haptischer Kauf.

_Thun: Haptik kommt aus der Arbeit mit den Fingern. Als Linkshänder blättere ich von der letzten Seite nach vorne. Daher achte ich auf die Konsistenz des schnellen Blätterns. Liegt das Magazin gut in der Hand? Oder läuft es mir davon? Selbstverständlich muss auch ein schlüssiges Storyboard da sein. Es sollte stets eine Spannung vorhanden sein, die man von der letzten bis zur ersten Seite spüren kann.

Der jüngste Luxustrend ist nicht mehr, Inseln zu erwerben, sondern Grundstücke auf dem Mond[2] oder Mars. Wäre das was für Sie?
_Strehle: Für mich scheint er jede Nacht.
_Thun: Ich besitze ohnehin den ganzen Mond.

Aber nicht auf dem Papier, Herr Thun. /////

1 Strehle & Thun Teamwork: Für das Vigilius Mountain Resort entwarf Gabriele Strehle das Design der Personaluniformen. Die gesamte Architektur stammt von Matteo Thun.

2 Exklusiver Verkauf von extraterrestrischen Grundstücken [Mond, Mars, Venus] unter: www.lunarembassy.com

Gabriele Strehle
In Süddeutschland geboren, tritt Gabriele Strehle 1973 nach einer Maßschneiderlehre und dem Designstudium an der Münchner Modeschule in das damalige Unternehmen Strehle KG in Nördlingen ein. Nur wenige Jahre später übernimmt sie die kreative Gesamtverantwortung. Zusammen mit ihrem späteren Mann Gerd Strehle entwickelt sie aus der vormaligen Mantel- und Kostümfabrik ein modernes, internationales Unternehmen, die Strenesse AG. Gabriele Strehle zählt heute zu den erfolgreichsten deutschen Modeschöpfern und erzielt mir ihrer Arbeit internationale Anerkennung.

⇒ Aktuelles Projekt: Strenesse Menswear Collection 2003/2004
⇛ Strenesse AG, Eichendorffplatz 3, D-86720 Nördlingen
T. +49.9081.807.0, www.strenesse.com

Matteo Thun
Matteo Thun ist im Jahre 1952 in Süd Tirol geboren. An der Salzburger Akademie studierte er unter Oskar Kokoschka. 1975 graduierte er als Architekt an der Universität von Florenz. Zusammen mit Ettore Sottsass gründete Matteo Thun 1980 den "Memphis Design Group". Zwischen 1983-1996 lehrte Matteo Thun als Professor an der Universität in Wien. Im Jahre 1984 eröffnete Matteo Thun sein Designatelier in Mailand. Heute besteht das Atelier aus einem Team von 50 Architekten, Designern und Graphikern, die für internationale Kunden tätig sind.

⇒ Vigilius Mountain Resort [siehe auch Seite 42]
⇛ Matteo Thun, Via Appiani 9, I-20121 Milano
T. +39.02.6556911, www.matteothun.com

Optionale Architektur Instant Balcony

Die Architekten Malte Just und Till Burgeff befriedigen einen Wunsch des urbanen Wohnens mit einem aufblasbaren Balkon, der an jedem Fenster befestigt werden kann. Beim nächsten Umzug wird er einfach mitgenommen. Wir haben mit den Erfindern gesprochen.

Altbauwohnung, Parkett, Tageslichtbad, Stuck, kernsaniert. Kann einem da noch etwas fehlen?
_Malte: Jetzt nicht mehr. Ein Balkon ist ja nun jederzeit möglich. Optionale Architektur nennen wir das. Du kannst es auch optionalen Luxus nennen.

Also du würdest schon sagen, dass ein Balkon Luxus ist?
_Malte: In jedem Fall ist es unser "Instant Balcony" Luxus. Der ist schließlich nicht nur einfach da, sondern er kann mal da sein und mal nicht. Luxus nach unserem Verständnis lebt von Möglichkeiten.

Beschreibe uns das mal. Wir wollen jetzt auf dem nicht vorhandenen Balkon frühstücken. Wie geht das?
_Till: Er kommt in einer Box. Dann muss man ihn einfach auffalten, mit den Gurten am Fenster befestigen, aufblasen, fertig. Der Balkon ist mit 240 kg belastbar, beschädigt nicht die Fassade und fällt auch ganz sicher nicht runter. Ich nehme den "Instant Balcony" und suche das Fenster aus, wo die Aussicht am schönsten und die Sonne am angenehmsten ist. Da kommt er hin. Zumindest heute. Morgen vielleicht an einem anderen Fenster. Vielleicht willst du ja auf der anderen Seite des Hauses in der Abendsonne den trockenen Chardonnay trinken.

Wir sind gespannt auf die ersten, die wir sehen.
_Malte: Wenn ihr sie nicht seht, heißt das nicht, dass sie nicht da sind. Vielleicht ist der Besitzer gerade unterwegs zu einem balkonlosen Freund. Doch in naher Zukunft wird man in Grossstädten hier und da den einen oder anderen Instant Balcony entdecken, da wir momentan mehrere Gespräche mit Investoren führen, die den Instant Balcony in Serienproduktion geben wollen.

Technische Informationen zum Instant Balcony
Aufblasbarer Balkon
Max. Tragfähigkeit: 240 kg
3-Punkt-Sicherheits-System
Aus strapazierfähigen Textilien und Neopren
Maße: 1,5 x 2,5 m

Zuerst wird die Mittelkammer des Instant Balcony zur Stabilisierung der Konstruktion in der Fensterlaibung aufgeblasen. Für die Klemmwirkung zum festen Halt des Balkons an der Fassade werden der innere und äußere Ring mit Druckluft aufgeblasen und gegeneinander mit Gurten verzurrt. Instant Balcony klemmt sich fest, ohne die Fassade zu beschädigen. /////

⇛ Just.Burgeff. Architekten
Mörfelder Landstrasse 109, D-60598 Frankfurt
T. +49.69.60607320, www.just.burgeff.de

Statik: Jürgen Scholte-Wassink

PHOTOGRAPHY BY
DARIUS RAMAZANI

ASSISTANT _HAMILTON PERREIRA
PROCESSING LAB _OPAQUE BERLIN, PIETRO GIRIBALDI

High Print Culture

Edelste Prägedruckkunst: Bölling Germany produziert die feinsten Akzidenzen der Branche. Geschäftsführer Marco O. Bölling über Zeit, Qualität und die Veredelung von Papier.

Warum haben Sie sich gerade diesem Metier verpflichtet?
_Diese exquisite Nische des graphischen Gewerbes wurde von meinem Vater bewußt und mit außergewöhnlicher Weitsicht gewählt. Ihn reizte die schier unendliche Bandbreite der durch Prägetechniken erzielbaren Effekte, die sich mit einem ausgewählten Maschinenpark erzeugen lassen. Mein Eintritt in das Unternehmen hat die gleiche Begeisterung zum Grund: 08/15 kann auf die Dauer nicht ausfüllen ...

Qualität braucht Zeit. Zeit ist Geld. Die Bölling Akzidenzen sind ein teurer Luxus.
_Für den einen ist es eine Pflicht, für den anderen die Kür. Gibt es denn auch billigen Luxus? Nein, im Ernst: Es geht mit der Definition von Luxus einher. Betrachtet man Luxusgüter als Überflüssiges, das man sich erst leistet, wenn man die rationalen und nötigen Käufe erledigt hat, so muß ich widersprechen. Unsere Drucksachen sind sicherlich im Premium-Segment angesiedelt. Ist denn aber jemand, der Wert auf Qualität legt, per se ein Luxuskonsument?

Stahlstich- und Heißfolienprägung kennt man eher von Briefmarken oder Geldnoten.
_Prägen ist nicht nur individuell, sondern fälschungssicher. Natürlich beinhaltet die Herstellung von Geldscheinen noch eine Menge weiterer Merkmale, die über das Prägen hinausgehen, doch auch mit Einführung des Euros ist unseren Geldscheinen noch der Stichtiefdruck (ähnlich der Stahlstichprägung) und die Heißfolienprägung mit Hologramm geblieben. Diese Techniken kann man auch für die Produktion von Genußscheinen, Aktien, Tickets oder Clubkarten einsetzen.

Bei der Blindprägung wird bewusst auf Farbe verzichtet. Gilt auch hier auch das Prinzip: Weniger ist mehr?
_Ganz und gar. Nach der Theorie handelt es sich um das einfachste Verfahren. Die Tücke steckt jedoch im Detail. Blindprägen ist viel mehr als bloße Deformation des Bedruckstoffes. Die Wirkung entsteht durch scharf definierte Kanten oder fließende Formen, durch das Spiel von Licht und Schatten, durch Haptik und Dreidimensionalität.

Momentan stagnieren weltweit die Umsätze. Geiz ist geil. Gilt das auch für Prägedrucksachen?
_Sicherlich, aber wir halten es mit John Ruskin, welcher schon im 19. Jahrundert treffend bemerkte: "Es gibt kaum etwas auf der Welt, das nicht irgend jemand ein wenig schlechter und billiger verkaufen könnte, und die Menschen, die sich nur am Preis orientieren, werden die gerechte Beute solcher Machenschaften". Wir sind der Überzeugung, daß der Ärger über minderwertige Qualität nachhaltig ist. Wenn Sie einen minderwertigen Toaster kaufen, ärgern Sie sich vielleicht bei jedem Toastvorgang. Das mag schlimm sein, und Sie werden sich sicherlich bald einen hochwertigeren Toaster kaufen. Bei Ihren Akzidenzen ist das anders: Es steht Ihr Name darauf.

Welchen Beitrag leistet Bölling, um dem Prädikat "high print culture" gerecht zu werden?
_Es geht um Kunst und Kultur, nicht etwa um industrielle Massen(ab)fertigung – eben "Kunst-Hand-Werk" in seiner wahrsten Bedeutung. Unser Beitrag ist dessen Erhalt in tagtäglicher Anwendung. Es ist eine große Versuchung, Wertschöpfung durch Kostensenkungen zu steigern: geätzte Prägeplatten statt Handgravuren, schneller laufende Maschinen aus den USA, schnelltrocknende Farbe ohne Glanz – nicht mit uns. Der Anteil der Handarbeit an unseren Drucken ist so hoch, wie sicherlich in keinem anderen Unternehmen. Das fängt bei der Gravur an und endet erst dann, wenn die von Hand verlesenen Drucksachen gezählt und verpackt sind. Anachronistisch ist unser Arbeiten trotzdem nicht. Modernste Technik setzen wir überall dort ein, wo sie zu einer Verbesserung der Qualität oder Abläufe dient, zum Beispiel in der Vorstufe oder im wasserlosen Offsetdruck.

Bölling im Jahre 2023 – trotz digitaler Revolution?
_Selbstverständlich! Nachdem die digitale Hysterie nun in sinnvolle Bahnen gelenkt wird und man langsam erkennt, wo welche Technik gewinnbringend (und das meine ich nicht nur monetär) eingesetzt werden kann, erwarte ich eine Renaissance der "Füllfedernutzer" und "Briefeschreiber". Die jüngsten Ergebnisse einer Befragung von Art Direktoren weist in die richtige Richtung: Haptik ist ein wesentliches Mittel der Kommunikation.
/////

Marco O. Bölling
Leitet das operative Geschäft von Bölling Germany seit 1998. Das Unternehmen wurde 1964 von Karlheinz Bölling gegründet. Es folgten Partnerschaften in den USA und Akquisitionen in Deutschland. 7 Mitarbeiter zählt die Firma zum festen Stamm, daneben mehrere Freelancer und hochqualifizierte Graveure.

⇛ Bölling Germany, Schwalbacher Str. 83, D-65812 Bad Soden
T. +49.6196.76698.0, www.boelling.com

ABC Deluxe

„Bald werden Unternehmen die Länder ersetzt haben. Dann ist man nicht mehr Bürger einer Nation, sondern Markenbewohner, lebt in Microsoftien oder Mcdonaldland, ist Calvin Kleiner oder Pradaese.“ *(Frédéric Beigbeder, 39,90, www.rowohlt.de)*

Ja, und wir buchstabieren nicht mehr nach dem NATO Buchstabieralphabet oder A wie Anton, sondern nach Luxusmarken, dem ABC Deluxe.

A	ARMANI	N	NIKE
B	BOTTEGA VENETA	O	ORIGINS
C	CHANEL	P	PRADA
D	DE BEERS	Q	QUÉBEC
E	ETRO	R	RIVA
F	FERRARI	S	STRATO
G	GUCCI	T	TIFFANY
H	HERMÉS	U	UNGARO
I	ICEBERG	V	VERTU
J	JAGUAR	W	WEINECK COBRA
K	KIEHL'S	X	XAVIER DELCOUR
L	LOUIS VUITTON	Y	YVES SAINT LAURENT
M	MOËT CHANDON	Z	ZANOTTA

PHOTOGRAPHY BY
PIERO BORSELLINO

HAIR BY
VISSANI HAIR _FRANCESCO D'ANGELO, TERRY & ANTONELLA

STYLING & MAKE UP _KILLS.DE
PROCESSING LAB _WWW.FOTOQUICK-LABOR.DE
MODELS WEAR EXCLUSIVELY _AMERICAN APPAREL.
WWW.AMERICANAPPAREL.NET
VISSANI HAIR _T. +49.69.886346

WAS BESITZT DU? AUF WAS KANNST DU VERZICHTEN? WAS HÄTTEST DU NOCH GERNE? WAS WILLST DU AUF KEINEN FALL MISSEN?

MODEL _MIRIAM. MAKE UP _CHANEL LÈVRES SCINTILLANTES-PIN UP.
_CALVIN KLEIN COLORS WATER LILY. _LANCÔME FLUIDE ILLUMINATEUR.

WAS ICH NICHT HABE?
ICH HABE KEIN DICKES BANKKONTO, KEIN STUDIUM, KEINEN FREUND, KEIN 170 M^2 LOFT, KEINEN BOXTER, KEIN FERIENHAUS, KEIN SUPERWISSEN, KEINEN J-LO HINTERN, KEINE KINDER UND KEINE ZEIT.
UND ICH HABE KEIN PROBLEM DAMIT. DAFÜR HABE ICH VIELE GEHEIMNISSE, FRAGEN UND UNENDLICH VIELE IDEEN.

MODEL _NICOLE. MAKE UP _YSL LISSE EXPERT. _YSL GLOSSY NAILS. _YSL LIPMARKER. _LANCÔME BLUSHPAPER NACRÉ. _MAGICILS TURQUOISE MAGIC. JEWELLERY _RED RING BY N:JOI.

ICH BESITZE EINE EIGENTUMS-
WOHNUNG IN ROM, EINEN
BMW Z4, EINEN WEIMARANER
UND EIN V70 VON MOTOROLA.
ICH KAUFE EIN BEI BERGMAN
UND GEHE ZU VISSANI HAIR.
MEIN NEUES IPOD CASE IST VON
JIL SANDER. ICH ACHTE AUF
JEDES DETAIL. SNEAKERS, DIE
MIT MEINEN INITIALIEN
CUSTOMIZED WURDEN ODER
ANDERE LIMITIERTE PRODUKTE,
SIND FÜR MICH DER AUSDRUCK
MEINER INDIVIDUALITÄT.
MOMENTAN BIN ICH AUF DER
SUCHE NACH DEN NIKE SAFARIS.

MODEL _TANJA. MAKE UP _LANCÔME BLUSH FOCUS ROSE DOROTHY. _YSL LIPMARKER.
JEWELLERY _GREEN RING BY N:JOI.

SIE DENKT WOHL, SIE HÄTTE ALLES? DABEI HAT SIE DIE MEISTEN GEHEIM-TIPPS VOM MIR. Z.B. DAS NEUE EATDRINDMAN-WOMAN – KURZ EDMW – IN FRANKFURT. SEITDEM ICH IHR DAVON ERZÄHLT HABE, IST SIE JEDES WOCHENENDE DORT UND TRÄGT STOLZ IHRE, BZW. MEINE ENTDECKUNGEN ZUR SCHAU. ANYWAY. SIE IST MEINE BESTE FREUNDIN. UND ICH BIN FROH, DASS ICH SIE HABE.

MODEL _JULIA. MAKE UP _CHANEL VITALUMIÈRE-CLAIR FOR FOUNDATION.
_LANCÔME MAGICILS FUCHSIA MAGIC FOR THE EYES. _YSL GLOSSY NAILS.

MORGENS TRINKE ICH MEINEN JOSÉ INFUSIONS, EINE TEESORTE, DIE ICH LETZTENS BEI COLETTE, PARIS ENTDECKT HABE ODER DEN SIZILIANISCHEN BLUTORANGEN-NEKTAR VON DEAN&DELUCA, NEW YORK. SHOPPING IST FÜR MICH AUF ENTDECKUNGSREISE GEHEN. MEINE LETZTEN ENTDECKUNGEN SIND DIE STILETTOS VON PIERRE HARDY, DIE BRILLE VON MARKUS NIKOLAI, DIE CELINE TASCHE SILVER SURFER, DAS ARMBAND VON BEN AMUN UND DAS TOP VON AMERICAN APPAREL. UND FRANCO D'ANGELO IST DER EINZIGE HAIR STYLIST, DEM ICH MEINE HAARE ANVERTRAUE, UNTER VERWENDUNG VON KIEHL'S PRODUKTEN.

MODEL _ANGELA. MAKE UP _YSL TEINT ÉCLAT DE SOIE FOR FOUNDATION.
_CHANEL EXTRACILS-SUPER CURL-NOIR FOR THE EYES. _LANCÔME BLUSH FOCUS CARAMEL TOFFEE.

ICH BIN EIN NONSTOP TRAVELLER, HABE VIEL GESEHEN UND WERDE NOCH VIELES SEHEN. DER NACHTEIL BEI SOLCH EINER VIELZAHL VON OPTIONEN IST, DASS MAN ANSPRUCHSVOLLER WIRD. EINMAL BUSINESS CLASS, IMMER BUSINESS CLASS BEI LUFTHANSA. THE GRAY IN MAILAND IST MEIN ABSOLUTER DESIGNHOTEL FAVORIT ODER DAS GREAT EASTERN IN LONDON. MEINE FREIZEIT VERBRINGE ICH IM RIDERS PALACE, LAAX ODER IM VIGILIUS MOUNTAIN RESORT, SÜDTIROL. ICH WEISS GENAU WAS ICH HABEN WILL UND WAS NICHT.

MODEL _KATERINA. MAKE UP _CHANEL OMBRE UNIQUE CRÈME–HYDRA FOR THE EYES. _CHANEL DOUBLE CONTRASTE-PALM BEACH FOR THE LIPS. JEWELLERY _GREEN RING BY N:JOI.

Words Deluxe.

Anagrams are words or phrases formed by rearranging all the letters into new words. In this anagram all possible words used in the volume of luxury are taken in to consideration. An example: MYONE = MONEY.

NODDMISA _ _ _ _ _ _ _ _

PYTERORP _ _ _ _ _ _ _ _

ALVLI _ _ _ _ _

DGLO _ _ _ _

MRDEOEF _ _ _ _ _ _ _

Play&Win. Your solution? Langenscheidt LanguageMan.

WinLangenscheidt@M-Publication.com. Closing date: 30.11.2003. The course of law is excluded.

Luxury comes from above
In the Dolomite Mountains, 1,500m above the sea level, Mattheo Thun created the Vigilius Mountain Ressort, a new member of designhotels.com.

In purest crisp Alpine air, 1,500m above sea level, the Vigilius Mountain Resort is accessible only by cable car. No roads, no traffic, no noise. An exclusive refuge for a fortunate few, not all guests of the mountain will be guests at Vigilius. On the pristine Vigiljoch peak in South Tyrol, it seems natural that architect Matteo Thun should have been influenced by the strong surroundings. Like a tree that has fallen in the forest, the property combines old substance with fresh growth, generating new internal life and a commitment to renewal: 300-year-old timber beams, rich with history, have been resurrected in the Stadel-style restaurant. The grass-covered roof is an ultra-ecological solution to aesthetic energy conservation. Inspirational views of the surrounding Dolomite Mountains, with their ever-changing colors, act as the backdrop for "focus weeks" at the resort, concentrating on enhancing elements such as health, nutrition, movement and beauty. With exceptional autumnal interiors, exquisite Alpine / Northern Italian cuisine and a hedonistic spa, Vigilius Mountain Resort represents the bright future of elite hospitality.

Povera Italia

Or sono 25 anni che vivo sopra terra
e non si fa ancor altro
che parlare d'emigrazione.
Chi emigra di qua, e chi di la
lasciamo tutti la nostra città
chi in Germania, in Francia, in Svizzera
e chi in Canadà.
Siamo tutti sperduti in questo mondo
in cerca di guadagnar.
Povera Italia, Povera Italia
che ne sarà mai della tua Sicilia?
Adesso mi rivolgo un po
con il Signor Presidente
quello che sta a Roma a governare
o meglio dire senza far niente.
Caro Presidente, ti comporti male
perchè ai tuoi figli fai emigrare?
perchè far star loro, lontano
dalle sue famiglie, affinchè un giorno
scenderanno le lacrime alle sue pupille?
Povera Italia, Povera Italia
che ne sarà mai della tua Sicilia?
La gente del meridione l'hai scordata
tu te ne stai al Quirinale
e così godi la tua vita.
Ascolta la parola d'un tuo connazionale
ascoltami non farti pregare,
metti lavoro nel meridione,
e così i tuoi figli potranno ritornare

BY PASQUALE BORSELLINO

Povera Italia

Or sono 25 anni che vivo sopra terra
e non si fa ancor altro
che parlare d' emigrazione.
Chi emigra di qua, e chi di la
lasciamo tutti la nostra Cittá
chi in Germania, in Francia, in Svizzera
e chi in Canadá.
Siamo tutti sperduti in questo mondo
in cerca di quadagnar.
Povera Italia, Povera Italia
che ne sará mai della tua Sicilia?
Adesso mi rivolgo un po
con il Signor Presidente
quello che sta a Roma a governare
o meglio dire senza far niente.
Caro Presidente, ti diporti male
perche ai tuoi figli fai emigrare?
Perche far star loro, lontano
dalle sue famiglie , affinchè un giorno
scenderanno le lacrime alle sue pupille?
Povera Italia, Povera Italia
che ne sará mai della tua Sicilia?
La gente del meridione l' hai scordata
tu te ne stai al Quirinale
e cosi godi la tua vita.
Ascolta la parola d' un tuo connazionale
ascoltami non farti pregare,
metti lavoro nel meridione,
e cosi i tuoi figli potranno ritornare
ripeto non farti pregare.
All etá di 18 anni, io emigrai
e la mia bella Cattolica lasciai,
partii con un nodo al cuore
sperando che un domani
potevo ritornare,
e da quel giorno
sette anni son giá passati
e speranze di ritornare
mai ne ho vedute.
Ed ora mi sono rassegnato
pensando, che a quei tedeschi
come un cane mi hai venduto.
Povera Italia, Povera Italia
che ne sará mai della tua Sicilia?
E adesso chiudo per non farla esagerata
ma senza ai tuoi figli
che li all' estero
la vita la fanno sacrificata.
Si sacrificar la vita, non é pecato
ma tu sei stato , sempre bene in tanato
e al tuo portafoglio ai pensato
e di noi ti sei scordato
che all' estero ci hai mandato.

Novembre 1976

PHOTOGRAPHY BY
NICO HESSELMANN _FOTO-UNION.DE

Take a breath of 89,9% luxury

Oxygen is a gaseous element. It forms only 21% of the atmosphere of the Earth by volume while the atmosphere of Mars contains about 0.15% of this gas. It is invisible, inodorous, tasteless and compressible. Oxygen, which is very reactive, is a component of hundreds of thousands of organic compounds and combines with most elements. Plants and animals rely on oxygen for respiration. Medical research has indicated that oxygen deficiency for humans is probably the greatest cause of degenerative diseases like cancer, athesclerosis, diabetes and declining concentration levels.

Oxygen supports faster muscle recovery and is an energizing retreat. Inhaling oxygen can reduce emotional stress; can increase athletic performance, stamina, cure headaches and hangovers; can decrease cravings for alcohol and nicotine; can neutralize toxins, displace free radicals and destroy bacteria and viruses; can boost the immune system and promote cell regeneration; can help skin conditions, sleeping disorders, high blood pressure and premature aging. For other similar effects visit: www.M-Publication.com

ELIXIRSTUDIO_FRANCE
MAROK_GERMANY
SUBAKT_FRANCE
TIGER_JAPAN
VASAVA_SPAIN
SWEDENGRAPHICS_SWEDEN

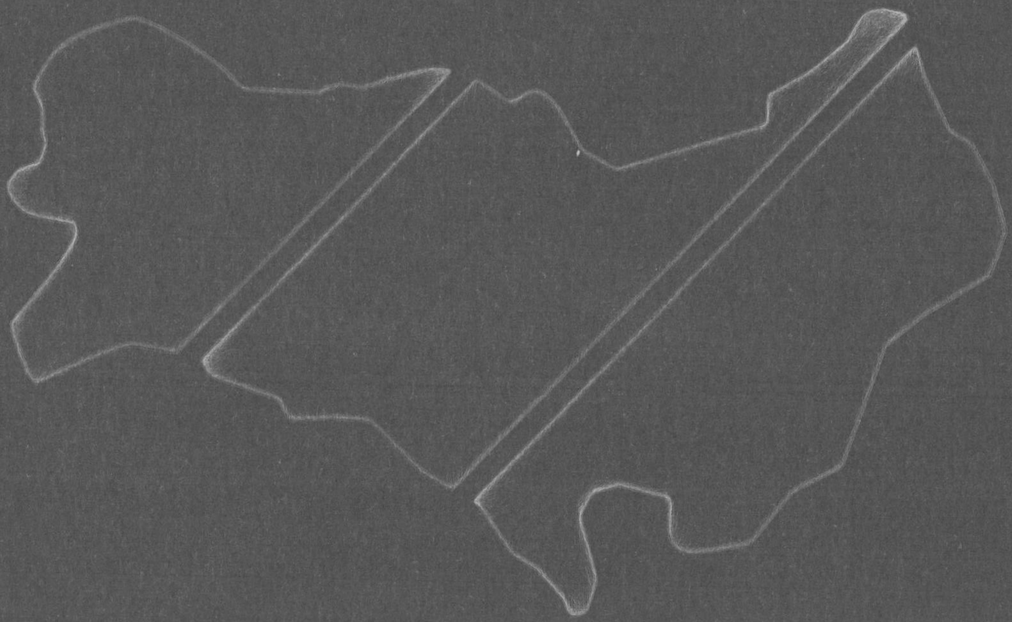

AN ASSEMBLY OF
DESIGNERS FROM
DIFFERENT NATIONS.
UNITED BY ONE
FORCE: THE LANGUAGE
OF VECTORS.

VEKTORIAT
IN COLLABORATION
WITH

MACROMEDIA

ELIXIRSTUDIO_FRANCE
MAROK_GERMANY
SUBAKT_FRANCE
TIGER_JAPAN
VASAVA_SPAIN
SWEDENGRAPHICS_SWEDEN

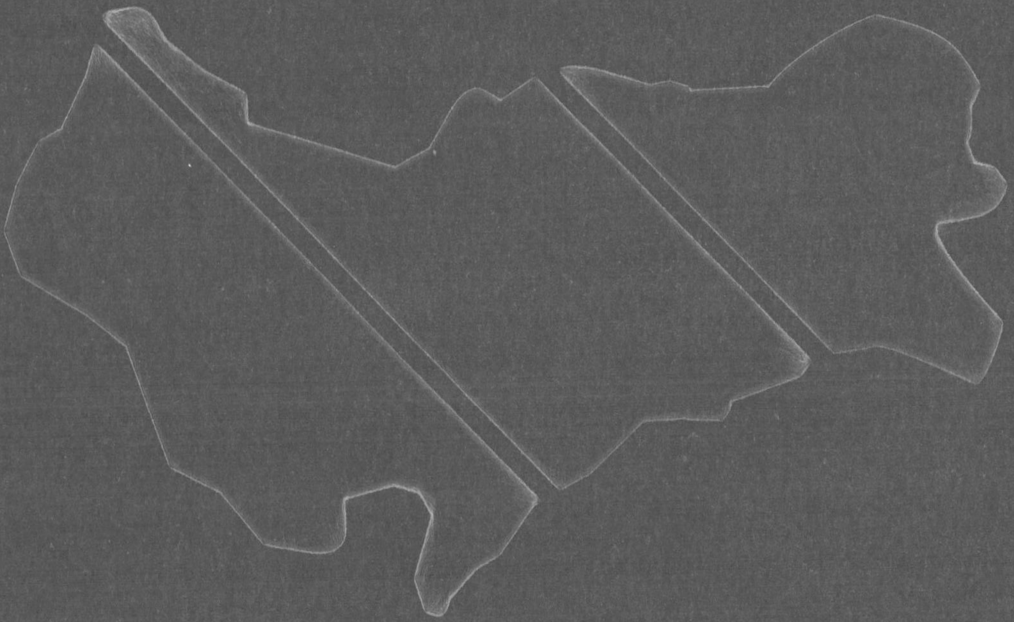

AN ASSEMBLY OF
DESIGNERS FROM
DIFFERENT NATIONS.
UNITED BY ONE
FORCE: THE LANGUAGE
OF VECTORS.

VEKTORIAT
IN COLLABORATION
WITH

MACROMEDIA

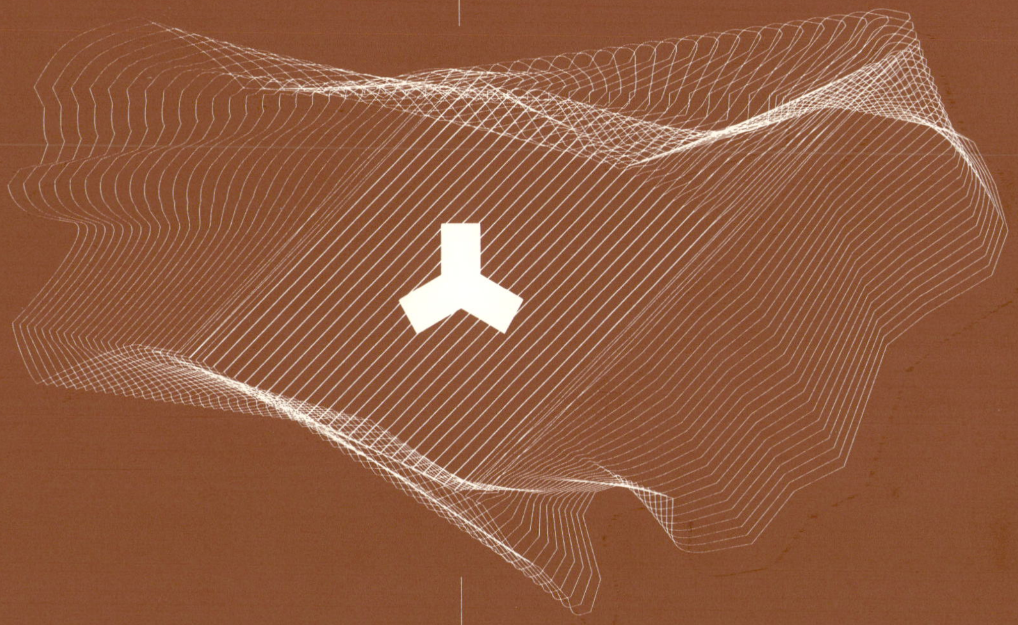

VEKTORIAT

IN COLLABORATION WITH MACROMEDIA

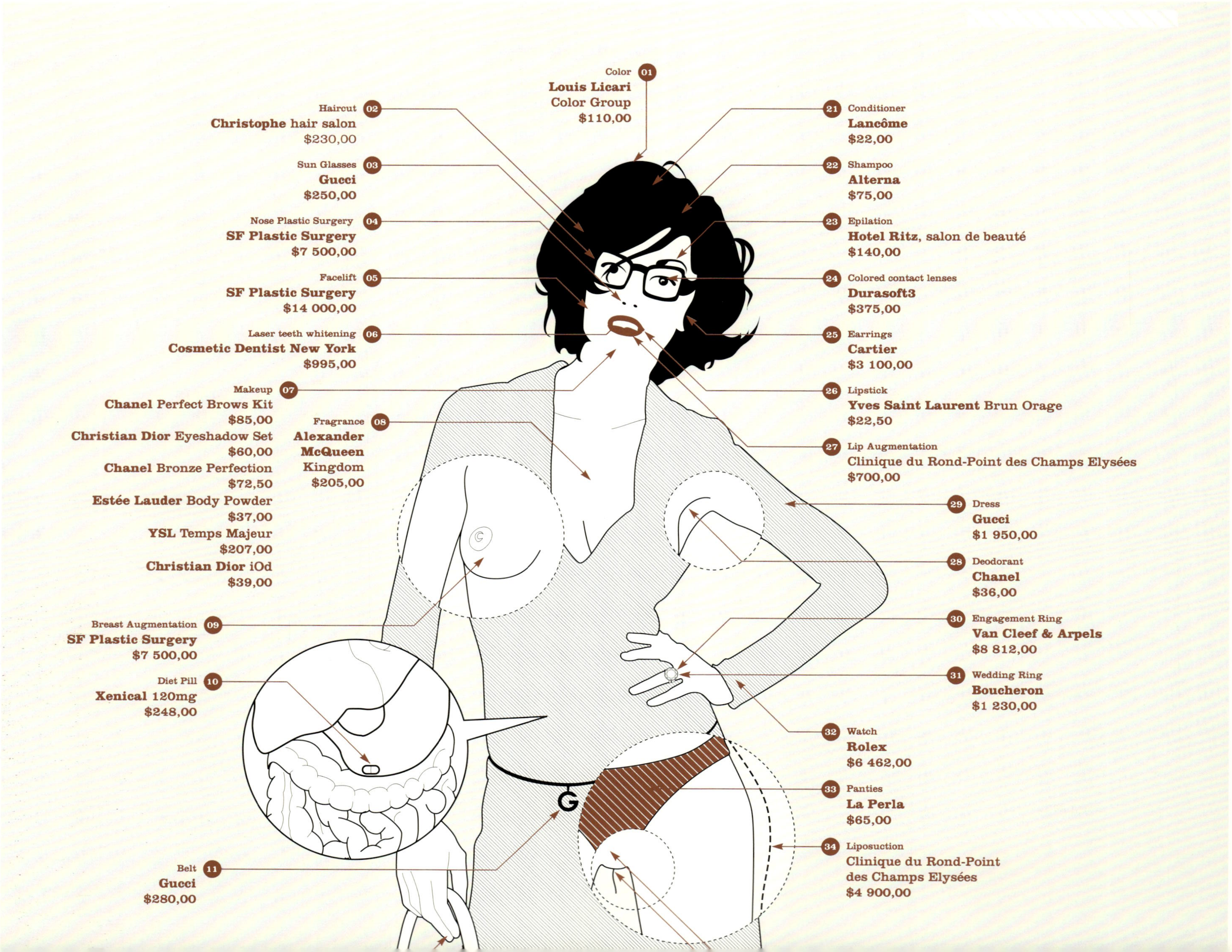

01 Color
Louis Licari Color Group
$110,00
02 Haircut
Christophe hair salon
$230,00
03 Sun Glasses
Gucci
$250,00
04 Nose Plastic Surgery
SF Plastic Surgery
$7 500,00
05 Facelift
SF Plastic Surgery
$14 000,00
06 Laser teeth whitening
Cosmetic Dentist New York
$995,00
07 Makeup
Chanel Perfect Brows Kit
$85,00
Christian Dior Eyeshadow Set
$60,00
Chanel Bronze Perfection
$72,50
Estée Lauder Body Powder
$37,00
YSL Temps Majeur
$207,00
Christian Dior iOd
$39,00
08 Fragrance
Alexander McQueen Kingdom
$205,00
09 Breast Augmentation
SF Plastic Surgery
$7 500,00
10 Diet Pill
Xenical 120mg
$248,00
11 Belt
Gucci
$280,00
21 Conditioner
Lancôme
$22,00
22 Shampoo
Alterna
$75,00
23 Epilation
Hotel Ritz, salon de beauté
$140,00
24 Colored contact lenses
Durasoft3
$375,00
25 Earrings
Cartier
$3 100,00
26 Lipstick
Yves Saint Laurent Brun Orage
$22,50
27 Lip Augmentation
Clinique du Rond-Point des Champs Elysées
$700,00
29 Dress
Gucci
$1 950,00
28 Deodorant
Chanel
$36,00
30 Engagement Ring
Van Cleef & Arpels
$8 812,00
31 Wedding Ring
Boucheron
$1 230,00
32 Watch
Rolex
$6 462,00
33 Panties
La Perla
$65,00
34 Liposuction
Clinique du Rond-Point des Champs Elysées
$4 900,00

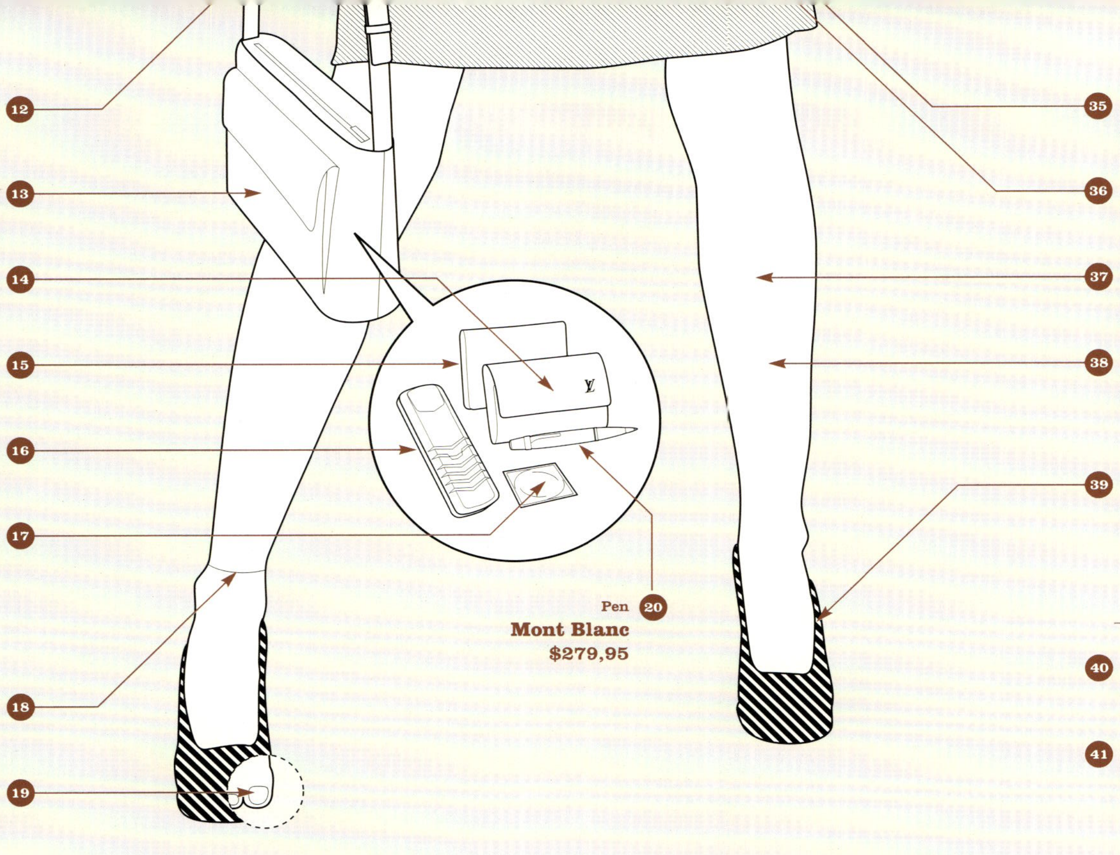

Miscellaneous

40 Styling Consultation
Kills.de
$3 640,00

41 Seduction Seminar
Robert Greene
$6 590,00

Grand Total

$97 431,87

What Women are Worth

The first international study of women's costs.

COPPERPLATEDRIMS | DESIGNER _MAROK, LODOWN.DE | NATION _GERMANY

moneyisrainingdownonmyarmouredbenzo.marok
copperplatedrims™

PAYMOBIL | DESIGNER _ARNAUD MERCIER, ELIXIRSTUDIO.COM | NATION _FRANCE

paymobil
SYSTEM

Inhalt
Contents
Contenu
Contenuto

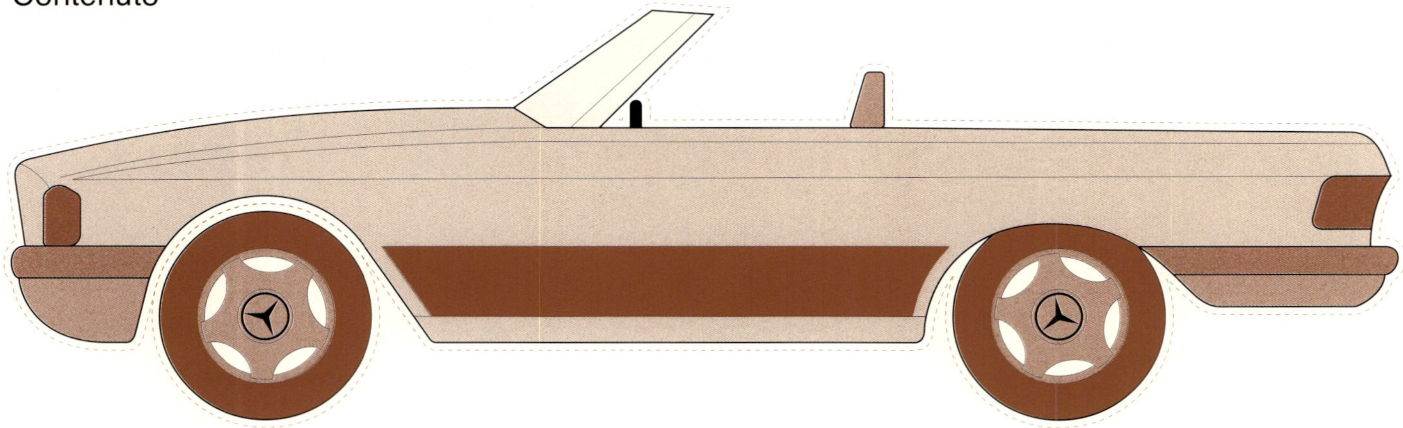

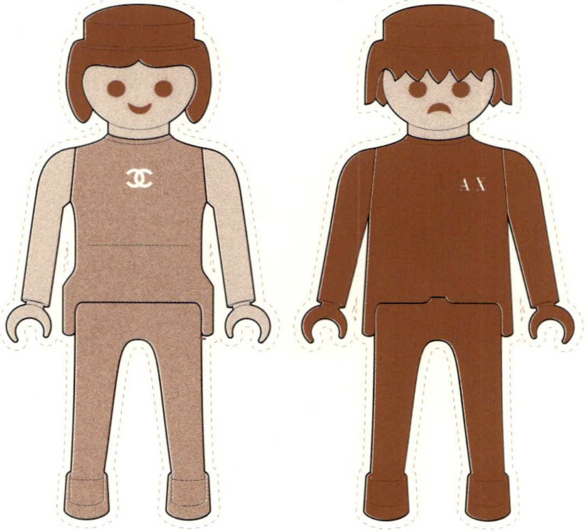

0876

elixirstudio™
limited edition

www.elixirstudio.com

2x

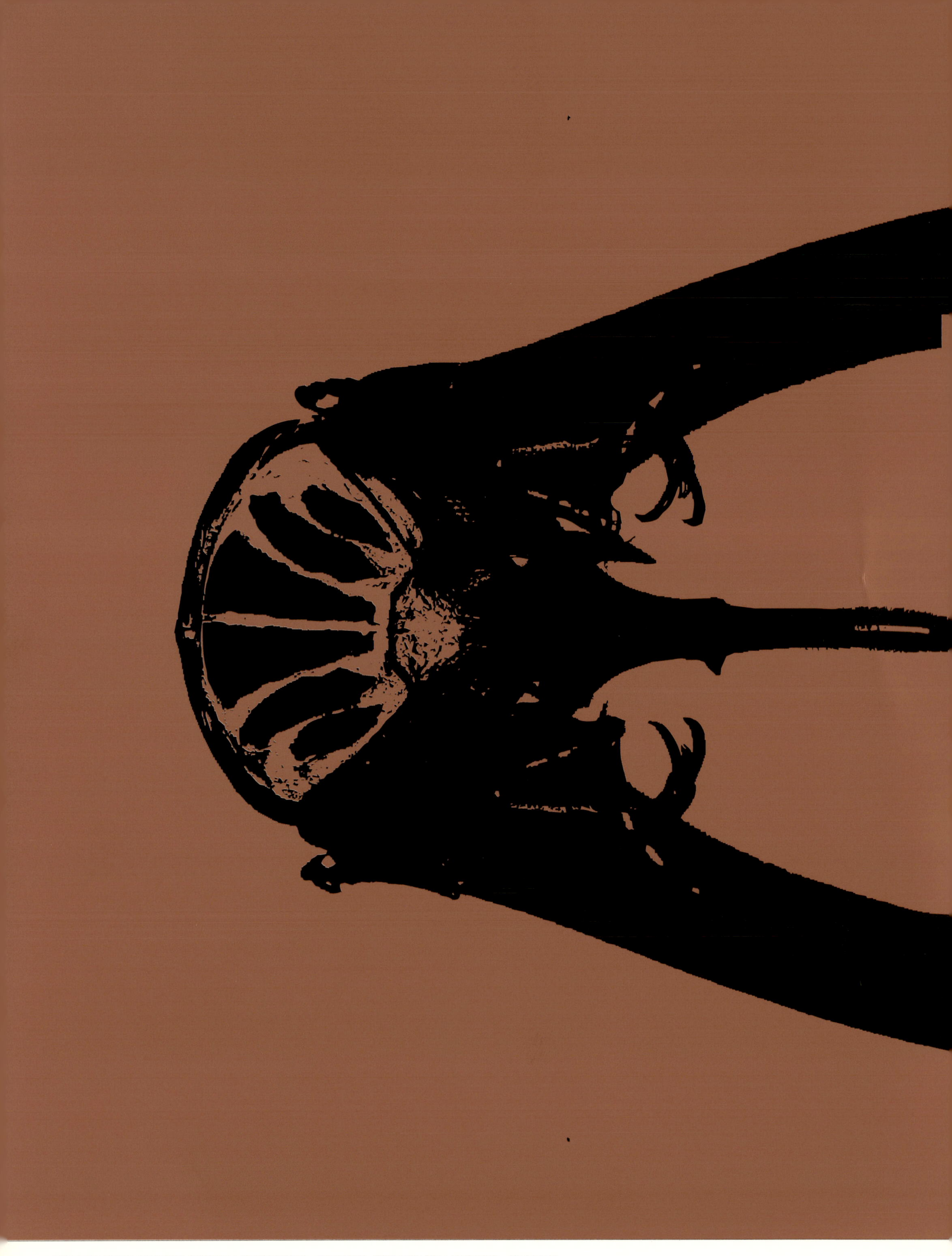

ENDANGERED SPECIES TREMA | DESIGNERS _SUBAKT, SUBAKT.FR | NATION _FRANCE

TRËMA
endangered species

A delicate melon perfume tormenting the Moroccan coffee merchant out on the corner of primrose and third. Often, though cold and chrome, her eyes make love on fur. Artificial fruit scents through the vents on the esplanade as we pass under the marble arch guarding entrance to the temple of Seven Pleasures.

FAUNA DELUXE | DESIGNERS _VASAVA, VASAVA.ES | NATION _SPAIN

vasava.es

THERE ARE STILL 86 KNOWN

KAKAPO | DESIGNERS _SWEDENGRAPHICS, SWEDENGRAPHICS.COM | NATION _SWEDEN

KAPOS LEFT ON THIS PLANET.

Luxury is giving up credit to things that seems superflous

Prisca Lobjoy, video artist

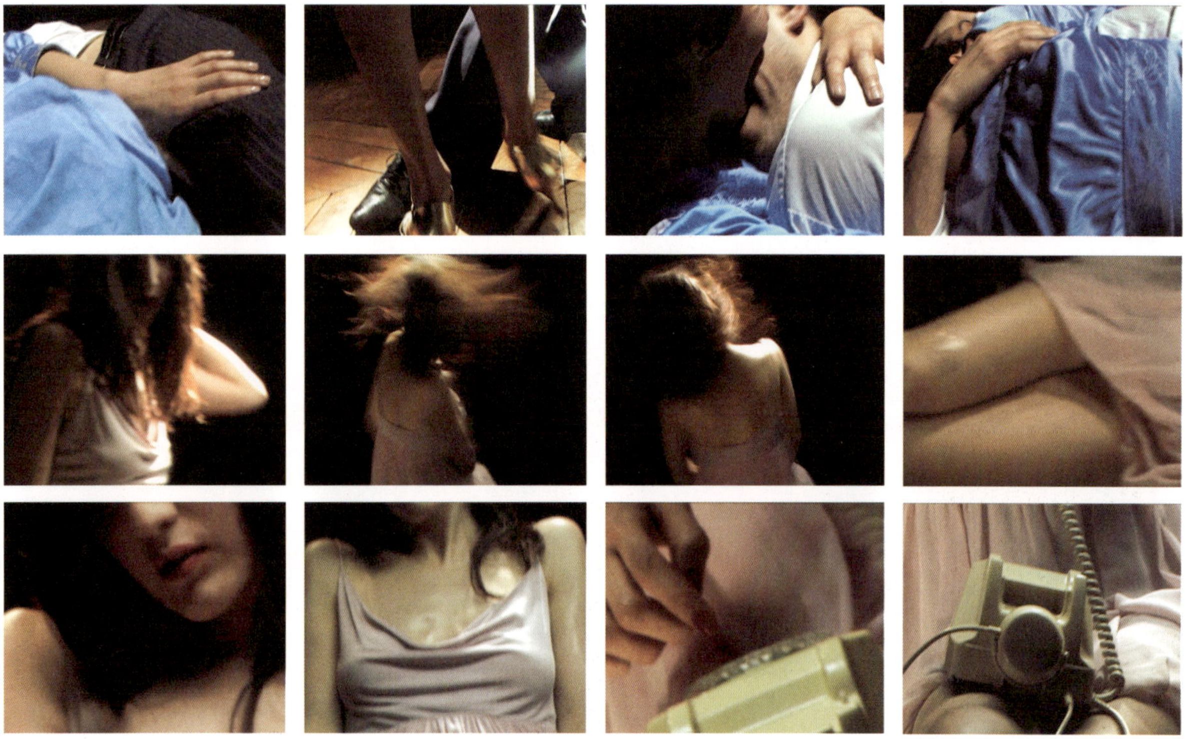

I asked Prisca Lobjoy what her thoughts were on luxury, and she said for her, luxury is not being a prisoner of a situation or a relationship, not being trapped by one's own body or mental habits. Luxury is experimentation. Luxury is giving credit to things that seem superfluous.

Prisca Lobjoy is in tune with the universe, she recognises and embraces its chaos and constant motion, and she knows that nothing stands still and everything changes. Motion creates motion, the continuous unstoppable flow of energy, the life force, the heartbeat, and the sex, the rhythms of the bass and drums, the tempo of human experience. She describes her approach to her work as that of a choreographer. Her pulsating loops of imagery dance across the screen like a free-falling dream, images appear and disappear in a heartbeat. She traces the movement of time using fragmentation and repetition, she plays with different levels of perception, nothing in her world is straight. Childhood memories flicker across the surface and are then lost to vibrant sexual imagery that twists and turns and pulses until it fades away or is interrupted by a different gaze. Prisca says she prefers to work with video as it allows her to work with movement and time and music, just like a silent film.

Out of the total darkness, the loud beating drums emerge with an electrifying energy.

Using the sounds of an unexpected storm and an invading army, the Gotan Project take their audience by surprise. Sirens sound and lights flicker, all eyes are fixed on the stage, time is suspended by the power of their electro voodoo dub magic.

Exactly on the beat, a cinematic horizon appears and the audience is engulfed by black and white loops of police and armies, and then by rioting crowds and chanting protesters. Here, the journey begins with memories of Buenos Aires and the dark side of Tango's past. Spellbound, the audience slips into the world according to Gotan, a world in which the senses quite literally collide, and each event is unique to that very instance and then washed away again into the ocean of memory. /////

The images above are taken from Prisca Lobjoy's new short film. See it at: www.M-Publication.com

⇛ www.gotanproject.com

The many luxuries of death

Death can mean many things – pain, grief, loss, sadness, happiness, joy and indifference. But death can also be luxurious.

PHOTOGRAPHY BY
CALLE STOLZE _LUNDLUND.COM

ESSAY BY
KRATHYN WHITE

The ancient Egyptians perfected the art, taking the idea of celebrating death with luxury to the extreme. Apart from the grand assortments of pickled people, animals, food and a whole lot of jewellery and furniture, the very act of pyramid-building, as a way for the spirit to attain closer affinity with the romantically titled invincibles – represented by stars in the sky – is nothing but luxurious.

And the idea of giving death luxurious overtones in the form of something beautiful isn't reserved to the ancient Egyptians. The ancient Incans had austere and beautiful burial practices similar to the Egyptians; Ghana's ornate coffins in the shape of spring onions; trumpets made out of human leg bones and a skull-hat made from human skulls originating in Tibet; grave makers from Madagascar; burial poles from the Tiwi Islands; gravestones of early Australian settlers placed in hill-top cemeteries overlooking the Pacific ocean; and life-size tua-tua wooden carvings made on the Indonesian island of Sulawesi to keep watch over the decomposing bodies beneath the earth.

Today, the story is slightly different.

Dousing death with luxury, like in ancient Egypt, is reserved for a select few - those with money or those with power. It could be a grand state funeral, a quiet celebratory cremation or a solemn wedding for two – the living lover and the dearly departed.

If you're a rich American, you could choose to have your remains cremated, capsulated and ejected into space, spending eternity orbiting the earth with the pile of other space junk. Or, for something more glamorous, you can now pay to have your body crushed into a gemstone resembling a large diamond to be worn around the neck or finger of a loved one. Gives new meaning to the term dead ringer.

But there are other, simpler ways death can be celebrated in luxury apart from hiring a hearse, getting a new black dress and selecting a well-appointed church with a gold-clad alter or spending a lot of cash getting your body crushed into cubic zirconia-like jewellery.

You could plant a memorial garden or memorial tree; set the ashes of a loved one free on the breeze over a field of wildflowers; make a book of moments celebrating the life once lived; or just being happy in the knowledge that with death comes the ultimate luxury of eternal rest. /////

ASSISTANT _CENGIZ BOZKAYA, VIDAR SÖRMAN
STYLIST _GUSTAF OLSSON _OBYGDEN
HAIR BY PETER ANDERSSON _MIKAS.SE FOR L'ORÉAL PROFESSIONNEL
MAKE UP BY KRISTINA KULLENBERG _MIKAS.SE
MODEL _KATARINA _STOCKHOLMGRUPPEN
LOCATIONS _WWW.SHOOTLOCATIONS.SE
CLOTHES BY _FRANK USHER. _E-PLAY. _EMPORIO ARMANI. _LAUREL. _TEMPLE.

PHOTOGRAPHY BY
DARIUS RAMAZANI

JOHAN NORBERG. MAY 2003 – KLEINMARKTHALLE FRANKFURT
STYLING: KILLS.DE. CAPITALISM-SHIRT: M-PUBLICATION.COM/M-SHOP

BY JOHAN NORBERG

Capitalism – the creator

Capitalism opened the doors for human creativity, giving us the opportunity of producing goods and services on an unprecedented scale – from starvation to a luxurious living standard. Still some people blame capitalism for the poverty in the world. To explore the reasons of poverty is of secondary importance, it is wealth that demands an explanation.

"Buy-nothing day" – leaving economic decisions to the people

Ideologists and thinkers fight over the best solution to our problems. Capitalism is the recognition that this one best answer does not exist. We can't build a perfect system which would suit everyone. That is why capitalism says that all peaceful ideas, projects and systems are welcome. It says that we don't know the one best way, so people have to decide themselves what might be best for them, what kind of ideas and dreams they want to realise and what kinds of goods and services they should or shouldn't consume. You are free to try anything, as long as you don't use force against other people, or force them to pay for your projects. Capitalism is the economic system that leaves the economic decisions to the people instead of the system.

Want a "buy-nothing day"? Sure, go ahead. You can have it every day of the week. Capitalism means voluntary relations. No deal is ever made if both parties don't think that they will benefit from it.

Some people blame capitalism for the poverty in the world. That's because they haven't studied – or at least haven't understood – history. Poverty is nothing new. Poverty has always been the fate of mankind. 200 years ago, every country was an underdeveloped country. The new thing in the world – the fantastic thing that demands an explanation – is wealth. The fact that some countries and regions have been lifted out of poverty for the first time in the world's history.

The reason is capitalism. It was capitalism that opened the doors for human creativity, so that we could produce goods and services on an unprecedented scale.

130 years ago, my forefathers in Sweden starved. Sweden then was poorer than Congo is today, and people lived twenty years shorter than they do on average in the developing countries. To survive, the Swedes had to make bread from bark, lichen and straw to survive, and they made porridge from meal minced from the bones of fish and other animals.

Sweden was not developed by socialism and the welfare state. If we had redistributed all the property and all the income in Sweden then, every Swede would be living on the same level as the average person in Mozambique. Instead, Sweden was liberalised in the mid-19th century, and free people in free markets with free trade could produce wealth, and make us a rich country. Our economy was specialised and made more efficient so that we could feed ourselves and afford other goods as well – clothes, housing, newspapers, education. By 1950, before the Swedish welfare state was built, the Swedish economy had quadrupled. Infant mortality had been reduced by 85 per cent and life expectancy had increased by a miraculous 25 years.

Regions divided not by people, culture or tradition, but by their political economy

This has happened in every place where people have the freedom to own, produce and trade – where they have capitalism. We can see this clearly in regions divided not by people, culture or tradition, but by their political economy. Capitalist West Germany became one of the world's leading economies, communist East Germany stagnated; capitalist South Korea went from underdeveloped to European standards of living, socialist North Korea went from bad to much, much worse; the Chinese in capitalist Taiwan had the fastest growth rate in the world, the Chinese in red China starved – until they started their own economic liberalisation.

In the last 20 years, global economic growth has lifted 200 million people out of absolute poverty. It is true that there is a horribly unequal distribution in the world. But that is because of the unequal distribution of capitalism in the world. Those who have capitalism grow rich – those who don't, stay poor.

Constant change of luxury due to dynamics of capitalism

130 years ago in Sweden, luxury was having sufficient food for the day, and being able to give your children an education – something available only to the rich. Capitalism made it possible for ordinary people to get that. Then luxury became affording a car and a telephone. Luxury is that which is almost, but not quite, within reach. And the constant change and dynamics in capitalism change the concept of luxury constantly.

Luxury is relative. Luxury is that which we want, but rarely have access to. When I was a poor student with a lot of spare time, luxury was affording to eat out and drink expensive drinks. Today, luxury is having more spare time to sit and read a book over a cup of tea.

The incredible development under capitalism constantly makes us richer, and makes the goods we want available to new groups. And as we get richer and can afford the old luxuries, new goods that we didn't know about before become the new luxuries worth striving for. In North Korea luxury is still having sufficient food to survive the day.

Living standards that kings of 200 years ago could only dream of

Today, more than 72 per cent of those classified as "poor" in the US have a washing machine and one or more cars, 60 per cent have a microwave, 93 per cent have a colour television. The poor in the US have more of these things than the average American had 30 years ago. The poor in Western countries have a standard of living that kings couldn't dream of 200 years ago.

And this is because some people were allowed to take the first steps to luxury. When the first millionaires bought a car, the socialists derided it as a rich man's toy. But the rich people's car purchases gave resources to the producers, who could invest them in more efficient production methods which made the cars available to more people. The same thing happened with refrigerators, telephones, radios, medicines and education. If those who fought for material equality and against luxuries had won the day, these inventions would never have been developed, and the research that went into making them in a cheap way for the mass market would never have been subsidised by the wealthy people's purchases.

So much for those who complain that the introduction of personal computers and the Internet creates a "digital divide". Progress always starts somewhere with someone, and that is contrary to their demand for equality. If they had been present 50,000 years ago, they would have complained about the "elemental divide" that was created when some learnt to control fire, or the "transportational divide" when someone invented the wheel.

No tampons and toilet paper for the Communists

Goods and services are not trivial. They contribute towards making our lives good, comfortable and entertaining. Those who think it is superficial must ask themselves why people strive for them everywhere. The kind of goods that are perceived as luxuries in a society say a lot about that society. One of the reasons why the Russians hated the communist system was that it turned tampons and toilet paper into luxuries. The first thing many Afghans did after the Taliban dictatorship had fallen was to put on some make-up and listen to the music that used to be forbidden. If not even brutal dictatorships can control man's interest in the good life, what could?

But if we always want more and better things, isn't this a curse rather than a blessing? We strive for more wealth, but when we attain that we are not content. Instead, we merely continue to strive for even more. Does money really make us happier? A singer answered: "perhaps not, but I'd rather cry in a Rolls-Royce than on a bus". But that is to understate the case. It is not the money in itself that makes us happier. Instead, it is the knowledge that our lives can improve. There is something in human nature that brings us joy when we get something that is hard to come by. Luxury is lust and joy. Capitalism - through constant improvement and wealth creation - is the only system that regularly gives us that enjoyment by letting us come closer to and within reach of luxuries, and that gives us new ideas of new luxuries, with the hope that we will attain them in the future as well. Not for a small privileged class, but for all of us.

Cubans swim to the US, and not the other way around

In six years, two thirds of the Americans in the poorest fifth of the population climb to one of the top three fifths. And at the same time, the bottom fifth is constantly filled with new poor immigrants and students who are about to enter the same upward social mobility. That is why Cubans swim to the US, and not the other way around. The hope for a better future is perhaps mankind's most rewarding and important psychological gift. Champagne and caviar are a good symbol for that.

For many elitist intellectuals, this is merely a materialist hunt for superficial pleasures. But that's merely because they have their own pleasures and luxuries. Finding that rare book, listening to that great lecture or getting that title of professor. We all have our favourites. These intellectuals would be amazed by the diversity of pleasures that exist in a society. They should learn to appreciate some pluralism. /////

Johan Norberg
Born in 1973, is one of Sweden's leading advocates of liberalism and capitalism. After studying history of literature, philosophy and political science at Stockholm University, majoring in the history of ideas, Norberg graduated in 1999. Since then, Johan Norberg has been in charge of ideas policy at the Swedish think-tank Timbro and has been devoting his time to several book projects. His international best-seller "Das Kapitalistische Manifest", has been translated into eight different languages and recently into German by Eichborn-Verlag.

- Das Kapitalistische Manifest, Johan Norberg, Eichborn
- www.globalcapitalism.st
  www.eichborn.de

PHOTOGRAPHY BY
PIERO BORSELLINO

EWIGES LEBEN™

KURZE, INTENSIVE BESTRAHLUNG
WIRKT AUF MATERIE UND GEIST.
HEILT KRANKHEITEN UND
VERSTÄRKT DAS IMMUNSYSTEM.
2,3 FACHER EL-FAKTOR.
50 JÄHRIGER = 21 JÄHRIGER.

FLUGSPRAY™
NEW YORK—PARIS IN 6,2 SEKUNDEN,
INKLUSIVE 35 KG HANDGEPÄCK.
ERHÄLTLICH ALS 15 ML ZERSTÄUBER.
REICHT FÜR CA. 30 MOBILISATIONEN,
UNABHÄNGIG VON DISTANZ UND ZIELORT.

GEDANKENLESER™

ZUVERLÄSSIGER INFORMATIONSLIEFERANT ÜBER
DAS GEDANKENGUT DER GEWÜNSCHTEN ZIELPERSON.
DIVERSE AUSWAHL- UND FILTEROPTIONEN.
REALTIME UND SIMULTANÜBERSETZUNG DANK
SPRACHERKENNUNG VON 2.489 SPRACHEN.

ZEITFUNK™
DIE ZEITHERRSCHAFT
IM PRAKTISCHEN HANDFORMAT.
STUFENWEISE EINSTELLBAR.
5/4 BIS 16 JAHR-SCHRITTE.
TRI-BAND-FÄHIG. VERGANGENHEIT,
GEGENWART UND ZUKUNFT.

It's all about substance

Claus Sendlinger, CEO of Design Hotels Inc announces the "Era of the nonsumers", delivering new definitions of luxury for the travelling industry.

How would you define the term "luxury"?
_To me, the ultimate luxury is to know what is going on. I would like to be able to have access to information in order to make my life easier as regards finding what I am looking for – in a way, to be able to forecast the future so that I can work on making things more efficient in my daily business. Learning and understanding the present will help us to understand and explore our future. I believe that our access to information is still a luxury and not easily available to everyone. Of course, luxury is not necessarily having riches and possessions at one's disposal. Luxury could mean having access to clear water, to fresh air and to space.

How much would you be willing to pay for a glass of clean, clearest water?
_It is hard to put a dollar sign on these bare necessities and it depends on the situation you are in and where you want to buy the water – in a supermarket, a bar or on a sailing boat while you are running out of water.

Shopping in Milan, diving in the Pacific, racing in Monaco – is this still luxurious to do all this?
_This was indeed luxurious a couple of years ago. People saved up their salaries to be able to spend money generously. At that time, brands did not exist everywhere at the same time, so you made an effort to travel to a city like Milan or Florence to enjoy a shopping tour with like-minded friends. Today the thrill about the great shopping streets in the metropolis' is gone – if you are in Stockholm, New York or Moscow you are encounter the same brands. We value certain items when we don't have access to them or miss them in a way. Once these items are available in abundance, they seem to be of less interest. This is human nature.

Do consumers set other priorities in terms of luxury?
_Luxury is now more about substance, quality and relationships. These values are worth more than a red stripe on the back of a shoe. I think we are in the era of the "nonsumers", who spend money more consciously. Health and well-being are more important than a fifth pair of Gucci pants. The "nonsumers" consume brands only to a certain degree. Neither do they need brands as guidance nor to be a part of the high society. They are mature and quite certain about his role in society and of how to set his personal priorities.

Nowadays, a swimming pool, a sauna, a gym, a massage salon and a personal trainer seem to be the standards of a good hotel. Do you concentrate more on individual needs?
_From my point of view, our target group is no more interested in a "ClubMed" kind of entertainment or vacation which guarantees the same programme no matter where the traveller is. Our target group moreover appreciates the culture and traditions of a country. Being in Southern Tyrol means experiencing the culture of that certain place and not being simply a cog in a big piece of entertainment machinery. What we are doing is all about individualism. It is about connecting the traveller with the locality.

Imagine you lost all your riches and possessions.
_You can have it all. I would do exactly what I am doing now and start all over again. Riches and possessions can be regained. To a certain extent they make life easier, but there are other things that count more, such as a childhood memory. I will never forget the celebrations we had in 1974 when Germany won the World Cup. You see, this is something you couldn't erase out of my mind.

Is Vigilius Mountain Resort, member of "design hotels", a luxury project? A place for the rich and affluent?
_Wellness is a synonym for so many things nowadays. Pick any hotel and it claims to be a wellness hotel. It gets difficult for the traveller to differentiate the real from the disguise. But "design hotels" is delighted to present a hotel like Vigilius Mountain Resort. The owners, together with Matteo Thun, created a place for you to recharge your batteries; it is an energy retreat not for the affluent but for those who value quality, substance and relationships. And yes, it is affordable to everyone, if the person really wants to experience something different. Luxury is all about having options to choose from. /////

Claus Sendlinger
Born in 1963 in Augsburg. Through Co-Ordinates GmbH, which he founded in 1987, Claus Sendlinger became involved in lifestyle travel and innovative tourism products at an early stage. An example of this is the international brand "design hotels" which he co-founded, and which today represents around 100 of the hippest, best designed hotels globally. The creative network generated through design hotels formed the basis for lebensart global networks AG, also co-founded by Sendlinger, who is currently Chairman of its Executive Board. Within the company, Claus is responsible for strategic development, marketing and quality control. In 2002, Condé Nast Traveller placed him in their Top 50 list of world tourism experts, sharing space in the category of most creative and innovative international tourism entrepreneurs with only seven other people.

⇛ design hotels, stilwerk, Kantstraße 17, D-10623 Berlin
T. +49.30.31515540, www.designhotels.com

BY KIMBERLY LLOYD

We work to work

Rinzen is a Japanese word which has various meanings – sudden awakening, commanding, awe-inspiring. Rinzen, a 5-person design collective, works on a range of client and personal projects – in print and Web design, illustration, fonts, characters, animation and music. Their luxury is their indulgence in their work.

Your approach to design is being copied by many designers; are you aware of your impact on the design world?
_Every creative person develops with the influence of specific artists or designers; we all exist in a flux of development that started centuries ago, and it's everybody's duty to contribute their own personal vision and ideas towards the future of design. "Influence" is cool, but "imitation" is just lazy (and, ironically, ultimately works against the imitator). It's inevitable, and is best ignored; we prefer to just get on with producing our best work and not be affected by it.

Have you created your profession out of your hobby?
_Our profession is the result of concerted, hard-won lessons in the area of applied design; the schism of "personal" work and "professional" work is not something that we give credence to – personal vision is realised in the professional explorations of the graphic form. Every idea is usable, in some form or other, in professional projects. The discipline is to be able to take ideas and incorporate them seamlessly, appropriately, and convincingly – i.e. to communicate.

In the 1980s, access to the Internet as an outlet for art was limited. Do you consider the Internet as a powerful vehicle in your career?
_The Internet was definitely crucial in the exposure that Rinzen gathered early on, and continues to be the most immediately far-reaching forum for our work to be seen. It is not perfect, in the sense that it lacks the appealing qualities of print that we love (and specifically take delight in exploring), but for convenience it is the grand leveller. Furthermore, the Internet makes communication, promotion and "networking" infinitely easier for all areas of human endeavour (whether fair or foul). It's a small, small, smaller world.

You seem to be enjoying your artistic control to the full on a variety of projects. How come, while other designers suffer restrictions?
_Self-directed projects imply complete control over intention and execution. With client projects, the only difference is that you have no input into the initial parameters, other than that the goal is the same: completion of the brief to an optimum level of communicative success.

Viva la Vector - what does that stand for?
_It's a celebratory cry invoking the power and humbling versatility and mathematical precision of the almighty vector! Viva la Vector!

The Vektoriat initiated by M is a project in which different talents worldwide are united. Rinzen is the ambassador of this project for Australia. What is it important for an aspiring young designer to know?
_Young designers are best served by spending long, painful hours becoming conversant with their chosen tools so that they can render the medium invisible to the end design or graphic idea. This includes knowledge and mastery of the end delivery vehicle, be it print, the Web, or something else. The learning process is never-ending, but the more energy you invest in it, the freer you will be to execute in a manner only limited by your imagination.

Is it important for you to produce art for the sake of art or to make it functional?
_Everything is functional, even if that function is verbally inexpressible or abstract – you apply the visual languages in order to communicate in ways that written language can't.

Self-critical?
_As dreamers we are always critical of everything that fails to reach our heart's desire; as designers we are always critical of everything that fails to reach the individual goals of any project and the overarching goal of effective, compelling communication.

What does luxury, money and time mean to you?
Luxury is the ability to transform yourself. Money is a lever. Freedom is a gift you give yourself. Happiness is anywhere you find it. Time is the direction. /////

⇛ www.rinzen.com / www.sozi.com
www.vektoriat.de

Fort Wayne
Bible College

Luxus provoziert Neid

Wir denken selten an das,
was wir haben, sondern immer
nur an das, was uns fehlt.

Arthur Schopenhauer

PHOTOGRAPHY BY
AXEL THOMAE _KOMBINATROTWEISS.DE

POST PRODUCTION BY
ROBIN PRESTON _KOMBINATROTWEISS.DE

CABRIOLET
BMW Z4 _BMW.COM

BMW

Recuerdo de México

Regen. Ich kämpfe mit dem Wind um die Herrschaft über meinen Schirm. Das Wasser findet seinen Weg rechts, links, hinten, vorne an ihm vorbei. Makellos. Vor meinem Haus geparkt der Z4 meines Nachbarn. Wie immer. Und ich? Dreimal mit meinem Floh um den Block und nun fünf Straßen weiter geparkt. Würde nie seinen Wagen außer Sichtweite abstellen. Hat viel zu viel Angst, dass... Fährt so lange ums Karree, bis Platz wird. Der Wagen hat einfach alles. Alles, was meiner nicht hat. Navigationssystem, Dolby-Surround-Anlage, Servolenkung und, oh, einen riesigen Kratzer im Lack. Ja, das hat meiner alles nicht! Muss Grinsen. Die Haustür fällt hinter mir ins Schloss. Grinse immer noch.

Im Briefkasten Werbung. Ansonsten Rechnungen. Eine Postkarte. Von Sybille. Ach, das ist ja lieb. Palmen, Sonne, Strand. "Recuerdos de México." Überfliege den Text. Dabei immer zwei Treppen auf einmal. Toller Strand. Klasse Hotel. Superwetter: 28 Grad Celsius im Schatten, nicht eine Wolke. Nicht eine Wolke in Mexiko, wiederhole ich leise, spanne meinen Schirm zum Trocknen auf. Nicht mehr sicher, ob ich mich wirklich über die Postkarte freue. Zeigt mir nur, wie schön es an einem anderen Ort ist. Einem anderen Ort, an dem ich nicht bin.

Hatte nicht mal jemand gesagt: "Wie gerne wir uns beneiden lassen, zeigt jede Postkarte, die wir schreiben." Wer war das bloß? Fürchterliches Namensgedächtnis. Sybille wüsste das jetzt. Aber Sybille ist nicht da. Liegt in Mexiko am Strand.

Gehe im Flur an meinem Spiegel vorbei. Meine käsigweiße Haut leicht grünlich. Neid wuchert unter der Haut. Würde er, wenn ich ... Aber ich bin nicht neidisch. Wirklich nicht.

Der Kratzer im Lack meines Nachbarn. Muss schon wieder grinsen. Nur so. Mir genügt der Floh. Bringt mich von A nach B. Und, fast noch wichtiger, meinen Kleinen kann ich auch fünf Straßen weiter weg parken, ohne mir Sorgen um den Lack machen zu müssen.

Sybille? Strandurlaub in Mexiko? Will ich das? Ja! Sonnenbrand, Falten, Wucherungen auf der Haut? Und nur eine Ein-Zimmer-Wohnung??? Nur Sybilles Namensgedächtnis, darum beneide ich sie wirklich. Doch da lässt sich leider nicht dran kratzen. Aber Mexiko? Bin kein Sonnentyp.

Wende ich mich meiner übrigen Post zu. Merklich besser gelaunt. Ein Brief vom Reisebüro. Buchungsbestätigung. Zwei Wochen Rucksacktour durch Island. Da muss ich vor allem an eins denken: mein Adressbuch. Damit ich Sybille eine Postkarte schreiben kann. Sie arbeitet dann nämlich wieder. /////

⇛ Staatliches mexikanisches Verkehrsamt
Taunusanlage 21, 60325 Frankfurt, T. +49.69.253509
www.visitmexico.com

Neid,
eine von Missgunst bis Hass reichende Gesinnung gegen einen anderen Menschen wegen seines Wohlergehens oder wegen Werten, wie Besitz, Reichtum, Ruhm u.a., deren Besitz dem Neider nicht gegeben ist, ihm aber erreichbar scheint; eine vorwiegend negativ zu bewertende Triebkraft im Rahmen menschlichen Zusammenlebens, von zum Teil sehr zerstörerischer Kraft. Häufig strebt der Neider weniger danach, die beneideten Vorzüge zu gewinnen, als danach, dass der Beneidete sie auch nicht hat oder sie verliert – Schadenfreude.

Brockhaus, die Enzyklopädie, Band 15, Seite 466
Bibliographisches Institut & F. A. Brockhaus AG, 2001
www.brockhaus.de

NAME	BURST	ICON	HEMALIA	INTERMARINE
WERT	ca. 3.000.000 $US	6.750.500 $US	110.500 $US [Miete/Woche]	nur auf Anfrage
LÄNGE	24m	38m	57m	85m
EINHEITEN	2	3	4	5
DECKS	1	3	3	4

	1	2	3	4	5	6	7	8	9	10
A										
B										
C										
D										
E										
F										
G										
H										
I										
J										

	1	2	3	4	5	6	7	8	9	10
A										
B										
C										
D										
E										
F										
G										
H										
I										
J										

Yachten versenken

ILLUSTRATION
ALEXANDER SCHUKOWSKI

	THUNDERBIRD	ICON	MELODY	CARDINAL
	ca. 4.450.000 $US	7.580.5000 $US	98.500 $US [Miete/Woche]	Preis unbekannt
	39m	45m	51m	77m
	2	3	4	5
	2	4	3	5

	1	2	3	4	5	6	7	8	9	10
A										
B										
C										
D										
E										
F										
G										
H										
I										
J										

	1	2	3	4	5	6	7	8	9	10
A										
B										
C										
D										
E										
F										
G										
H										
I										
J										

PHOTOGRAPHY BY
DOMINIK GIGLER _KLOSSLONDON.COM

STYLIST _JULIANE KAHL
HAIR _KARL BERNDSEN _TERRI MANDUCA
MAKE UP _DAN HAZELDEAN _TERRI MANDUCA
MODEL _CAROLINE FARRINGTON _PROFILE
PHOTOGRAPHER'S ASSISTANT _MIKE HEMY

LEFT PAGE.
DRESS _ROBERT CARY WILLIAMS.
SHOES _BEYOND RETRO.
RIGHT PAGE. DRESS _PORTOBELLO MARKET.
PETTICOAT, SHOES _BEYOND RETRO.

LEFT PAGE.
OVERALL _PREEN.
SHOES _PORTOBELLO MARKET.

RIGHT PAGE.
LEATHER JACKET _PREEN.
NETSHIRT _PORTOBELLO MARKET.
LEGGINS _BIBI VOM PORTOBELLO MARKET.
SHOES _BEYOND RETRO.

ILLUSTRATION
JONAS BANKER _AGENTFORM.SE

Precious Moments

There aren't that many precious moments in one's short life. The very few that we experience can be counted on one hand: the first day at school, the first kiss, victorious moments, the first time we had intercourse, the birth of a child, and maybe the phenomenon of one celestial body that obscures the other, be it a lunar or solar eclipse. What all these moments have in common is that they are rare, and that makes them extraordinary in a way. This list might sound kitschy. M has left free space for your precious moments.

Luxury is a matter of having options

Things that could make you happy

01. Sharp Viewcam VL-Z5S
www.sharp.com

02. Yves Saint Laurent M7 Lotion Après-Rasage
www.ysl-m7.com

03. Strenesse Limited Edition Bag. 80 pieces worldwide.
www.strenesse.com

04. TDK XS-IV80 Multimedia Speaker System
www.tdk.com

PHOTOGRAPHY BY
PIERO BORSELLINO

STYLING _KILLS.DE PRODUCTS _GRAVIS TARMAC, KINGPIN, CIRCUIT.
_LEE JEANS AUTUMN/WINTER 2003. _LANGENSCHEIDT DICTIONARY. _LONGLIFE SUITCASE 1967.

Luxus bedeutet Vielfalt / luxury is diversity / Anti-Baby-Pille / Künstliche Befruchtung / Haarentfernungsmittel / Haarwuchsmittel / Zwangsernährung / Diät-Pille / Bewässerungsanlagen / Entwässerungsanlagen / Übergewichtig / Magersüchtig / Brille / Kontaktlinsen / Laser / Capitalism / Socialism / Laissez Faire / Marxism / Coca Cola / Pepsi / Afri-Cola / Fanta / Mirinda / Sprite / 7-Up / Buddhism / Islam / Christianity / Hinduism / OB / Tampax / Haute Cuisine / Fast Food / Luxembourg / Lichtenstein / Monaco / Cayman Islands / LanguageMan / Franklin / Beef / Pork / Kangaroo / Chicken / Veal / Nike Adidas / Reebok / Hi-Tec / Lee / Levi's / Diesel / American Apparel / Hanes / Fruit of the loom / Champion / Macromedia Freehand / Adobe Illustrator / Apple Macintosh / Microsoft / Frankfurt / New York / Milano / Persil / Ariel / Mcdonald´s / Burger King / Wendy´s / Taco Bell / Pizza Hut / Kentucky Fried Chicken / Gucci / Prada Black / White / Red / Green / Einfamilienhaus / Mehrfamilienhaus / De Niro / Pacino / Kubrik / Coppola / Schindler´s Liste / La vita è bella / Ferrari / Lamborghini / public school / private school / Nussbaum / Birke / Eiche / Ahorn / 69 / Missionar / Hündchen / Cunnilingus / Coitus Interruptus / Rose / Lily / Lavendel / Boutique / Mall / Concierge / Motorola / Vertu / Sharp / Monopoly / Pictionary / Scrabble / Marble / Ebony / Ivory / Nikon / Canon / to be continued...

PHOTOGRAPHY BY
MARCEL MEURY _FOTO-UNION.DE

PHOTOGRAPHY BY
DIRK MESSBERGER

Wissen ist Luxus

Die Wissensquelle in der edelsten Form: André Heller Brockhaus Enzyklopädie 2000, limitierte Auflage: 2.000 handsignierte Exemplare, Halbleder. EUR 12.782,30
www.brockhaus.de

PHOTOGRAPHY BY
DAMIANO CIRÀ

ZYKLOPÄDIE
2000
17
RAH-SAF
18
19
SAG-SEIE

Wenn Luxus redet: Das Qualitätsversprechen.

PHOTOGRAPHY BY
DARIUS RAMAZANI

ESSAY BY
JÖRG SKALECKI

PRODUCTION _DANIELLE GUIDET
IDEA _DARIUS RAMAZANI, JÖRG SKALECKI, IF-GROUP
PROCESSING LAB _OPAQUE BERLIN. PIETRO GIRIBALDI

Luxus ist die höchste Güteklasse der Begehrlichkeit. Man will ein Stück vom Superlativ, vom Besten, Seltensten, Reinsten und Originalsten. Wer diese Werte nicht kennt, dem wird gerne geholfen. Für die Güteklasse Luxus wurde eine eigene Sprache erfunden: das Qualitätsversprechen, das dem oftmals vermeintlichen Superlativ Stimme verleiht.

Wir haben das Produkt noch nicht berührt, nicht probiert, da verspricht es schon mit 100 % reiner Seide zu schmeicheln, lobt den traditionellen Familienbetrieb eines kleinen italienischen Pastaherstellers, proklamiert Seltenheit, stempelt Informationslust mit dem Hinweis auf Handarbeit und Reinheitsgebot oder trägt stolz Auszeichnungen längst vergangener Weltausstellungen zur Schau. Findet der Hersteller ein solches Argument selbst nicht, dann ruft er den Industriezweig des Marketing, der dem Gewöhnlichen das Luxuskleidchen des gehobenen Versprechens schon verpasst. Auf den ersten Blick. Unmissverständlich. Einprägsam. Zweifellos. Abgrenzung vom Gewöhnlichen als Ziel des Produktes im weltweiten Schlachtfeld des Angebotes.

Doch man ahnt es schon. Ein Versprechen macht noch keinen Luxus. Der Wunsch des Herstellers, sein Produkt in jene höchste Güteklasse zu heben und Begehr-

lichkeit respektive offene Portemonnaies zu erzeugen, endet oftmals in allzu offensichtlicher Durchschaubarkeit.

Wahrem Luxus reicht die Reduktion auf das Maximum. Ein Maybach kommt allein mit seinem Namen als Versprechen aus und auch Gucci hat ein "Haute Couture" unter seinem Label nicht nötig. Ein Château Pétrus addiert allenfalls ein "1921" hinzu, Chanel ein "No 5" und Intel ein technischen Luxus versicherndes "inside". Weniger ist mehr Luxus. Denn wahrer Luxus wird eben nicht durch Versprechen erzeugt, sondern erfährt nur eine feine Bestätigung. Das reicht.

Alles andere ist nur der Luxus, den sich die moderne Marktwirtschaft gönnt: mehr oder minder intelligentes Marketing.

Über dieser Betrachtung möge sich der Leser bei einem exzellenten Wein aus einem Swarovski-Kelch den höchsten Luxus nach einem Maybach oder wahlweise Bentley, einem hochkarätigen Diamanten oder einem niemals im Büro tragbaren Kleid aus der letzten Kollektion von Tom Ford gönnen: eine eigene Meinung. /////

Nicht zu viel, sondern zu wenig Globalisierung ist das Problem

Die Mythenkiller: Michael Miersch und Dirk Maxeiner über Legenden und Lügen bezüglich Globalisierung, Branding und Kulturimperialismus.

Reich werden in Deutschland ist richtig unanständig. In Ihrem Buch "Das Mephisto-Prinzip"[1] beschreiben Sie u.a. wie es Pädagogen schaffen, einen jungen Menschen ein für allemal zu versauen. Die treibende Kraft für jedes Individuum – der Egoismus – wird als eine große Sünde dargestellt. Unternehmerisches Denken und Handeln wird als das Ergebnis biographischer oder charakterlicher Entgleisungen wahrgenommen und die Suche nach Reichtum und materiellen Gütern als Irrweg abgetan. Warum?

_Miersch: Die alte Erkenntnis von Adam Smith[2], dass der Bäcker uns nicht die Brötchen backt, weil er uns lieb hat, sondern um Gewinn zu erwirtschaften, und dass viele Tausend egoistische Entscheidungen, wie die des Bäckers, den allgemeinen Wohlstand einer Gesellschaft mehren, klingt in Deutschland immer noch exotisch und revolutionär.

Wie lange kann das gut gehen?

_Miersch: Wir leben in einer Beamtenkultur und nicht in einer Kultur der Selbständigkeit. Das kann eine Weile gut funktionieren (und in Deutschland ging es lange gut), aber irgendwann sind nicht mehr genug Unternehmer vorhanden, um die Beamten zu finanzieren. Churchill hat mal gesagt (frei aus meiner Erinnerung zitiert): Sozialisten sehen im Unternehmer die Kuh, die gemolken werden muss, Kommunisten das Schwein, das man schlachten muss – doch sie sind das Pferd, das den Pflug zieht. In Deutschland kann man Abitur machen und ein Hochschulstudium abschließen, ohne je mit unternehmerischem Denken und unternehmerischen Tugenden in Berührung gekommen zu sein. Vor einiger Zeit habe ich mal das Ergebnis einer Umfrage unter BWL-Studenten gelesen und war echt erschüttert. Sie wurden gefragt, was ihr berufliches Ideal nach dem Studium wäre. Nur einige wenige reizte die Selbständigkeit. Die allermeisten wollten bei einem großen Konzern "unterkommen". BWL-Studenten! Also junge Leute, die noch am ehesten unternehmerisch denken.

In der wissenschaftlichen Studie "Economic Freedom of the World"[3] des kanadischen Fraser Institute wurden 100 Staaten der Erde nach den Kriterien für Reichtum und Armut, Freiheit und Unterdrückung untersucht. Heraus kam ein für manche Altsozialisten und Globalisierungsgegner provozierendes Ergebnis: Je kapitalistischer ein Land ist, desto reicher sind seine Bewohner. Wie definieren Sie Reichtum, Lebensqualität und Wohlstand?

_Miersch: Das Fraser Institute legt sehr vernünftige Maßstäbe an, und inzwischen tun das auch die Vereinten Nationen. Die fragen nicht nur nach dem Bruttoinlandsprodukt und nach dem Durchschnittseinkommen. Das kann in die Irre führen: Plötzlich stehen Länder gut da, nur weil eine räuberische, reiche Clique an der Macht ist, die über phantastischen Reichtum verfügt. Die Paläste Saddam Husseins haben auch das BIP im Irak gehoben. Andere Kriterien müssen hinzukommen: Lebenserwartung, Kindersterblichkeit, Alphabetisierung, Abstand zwischen Reichen und Armen. Diese Indikatoren geben Hinweise darauf, ob wirklich breite Schichten am Wohlstand Teil haben. Wenn man das alles berücksichtigt, kommt tatsächlich heraus: Je kapitalistischer ein Land (d. h. je freier der Markt in einem Land), desto besser geht es den Menschen dort. Harter Stoff für edle Seelen.

Farbfernseher, Personalcomputer, Internet, Mikrochiptechnologie, Weltraumtourismus sind einige der Fortschritte des 21. Jahrhunderts. Wie definieren Sie Luxus?

_Miersch: Luxus ist immer relativ. Wenn Sie in L.A. kein Auto haben, sind Sie arm. Wenn Sie in München kein Auto besitzen, kann das ein bewusst gewählter Luxus sein – denn Sie können mit öffentlichen Verkehrsmitteln alles bequem erreichen und müssen sich nicht mit dem leidigen Parkplatzproblem rumschlagen.

Herr Miersch, was sind die Standards heute und was bleibt noch Luxus?

_Miersch: Es wird immer neuen Luxus geben. Und das ist gut so. Was als Luxus anfängt, wird immer irgendwann allgemein erschwinglich. Aber am Anfang muss es teuer und prestigeträchtig sein, sonst gäbe es weniger Anreiz für Innovation. Die Erfinder, Ingenieure und Techniker möchten ja nicht ewig warten, um die Früchte ihrer Arbeit zu ernten. Also kosteten die ersten Mobiltelefone und die Personalcomputer richtig viel Geld. Unsere ganz normalen Wohnungen bieten mehr Bequemlichkeit als Versailles und Sanssouci, von der Bequemlichkeit des Reisens ganz zu schweigen.

Wie Sie in Ihrem Buch erwähnten, forderte die Expo-Chefin Birgit Breuel im Frühjahr 2000 zur Eröffnung

PHOTOGRAPHY BY
DARIUS RAMAZANI

DIRK MAXEINER & MICHAEL MIERSCH. MAY 2003 – KUNSTHAUS BREGENZ
ASSISTANT _HAMILTON PEREIRA. LABOR _OPAQUE BERLIN, PIETRO GIRIBALDI.

der Weltausstellung in Hannover dazu auf, "Intelligenz nicht zur Vermehrung bloßen Luxus einzusetzen, sondern sich darauf zu konzentrieren, wie die Früchte dieser Erde zwischen allen Erdenkindern gerecht verteilt werden können". Hat dann demnach jeder ein Grundrecht auf eine Eigentumswohnung?

_Maxeiner: Das Problem bei solchen politisch korrekten Sonntagsreden ist, dass sie so furchtbar substanzlos sind. Frau Breuel müsste ja zunächst einmal klären, was sie unter "Luxus" versteht. Eine Mahlzeit pro Tag oder drei? Ein Fahrrad oder ein Auto? Eine Urlaubsreise nach Mallorca? Eine Eigentumswohnung? Mit oder ohne Swimmingpool? Noch schwerer wiegt der zweite grundsätzliche Denkfehler in ihrer Aussage: Es wird gleichsam unterstellt, dass der Reichtum der Industrienationen auf Kosten der Dritten Welt geschaffen wird. Frei nach dem Vulgärmotto: Was der eine bekommt, muss dem anderen weggenommen werden. So funktioniert die Schaffung von Wohlstand aber nicht. Ideen und Fleiß schaffen Werte und Wachstum. Semireligiöse Verzichtsappelle laufen vollkommen ins Leere. Es gilt der Satz: Sankt Martin teilte seinen Mantel entzwei, woraufhin es einen Heiligen mehr, aber keinen Armen weniger gab. Selbst wenn alle Deutschen kollektiv Askese üben und alle Autos und die Industrie komplett abschaffen würden, würde durch diese heroische Tat kein Kind auf der Welt weniger verhungern, kein junger Mensch einen Arbeitsplatz erhalten und keine Tierart gerettet.

Worauf sind die armen Länder angewiesen?

_Maxeiner: Die armen Länder sind dringend darauf angewiesen, dass sie den reichen Nationen ihre Waren verkaufen können und dass wir als Touristen dort unser Geld lassen. Eine Verbesserung der Verhältnisse in Entwicklungsländern durch Mehrung unseres Reichtums mag moralisch misslich sein, sie macht aber ökonomisch viel mehr Sinn.

Ständig gibt es Diskussionen: Konsum ja – Konsum nein. Dem Konsumenten wird ein schlechtes Gewissen bezüglich dessen eingeredet, wie und wofür er sein Kapital ausgibt. Wie kann er sich denn so einen großen Mercedes kaufen und dann auch noch beim Bösewicht Shell tanken? Wem kommt das Konsumieren denn eigentlich zugute, dem Konsumenten selbst oder den bösen, habgierigen, kapitalistischen Industriellen? Oder kommt das Konsumieren dem Staate zu gute?

_Maxeiner: Es kommt letztendlich allen zugute, darin liegt ja der Erfolg der kapitalistischen Wirtschaftsweise. Das System mag nicht perfekt sein, aber es ist immer noch das beste, das wir haben. Es steht ja jedem frei, auf Konsum zu verzichten, und in dem ein oder anderen Bereich tut das ja auch fast jeder. Man sollte nur keine Moral daraus machen, das geht immer schief. Und man sollte nicht vergessen: Menschen, die konsumieren, die etwas kaufen und besitzen können, haben etwas zu verlieren und keine Lust, Kriege zu führen. Thomas Freedmann hat die friedenstiftende Wirkung von Konsum mal provokant als "Pax Big Mac" veranschaulicht: Keine zwei Nationen mit McDonald's-Filialen haben je Krieg gegeneinander geführt.

Im dritten Kapitel Ihres Buches schildern Sie, was sich in Tansania Anfang der achtziger Jahre abgespielt hat: Benzin war rar, Seife eine Kostbarkeit, Zigaretten wurden einzeln gehandelt. Fleisch und Gemüse waren knapp und teuer. Das einzig Funktionierende war der Schwarzmarkt. Dieser Zustand wurde als Dorf-Sozialismus schöngeredet. Wovor wollen Globalisierungsgegner wie z. B. deutsche PDS-Sozialisten, rechtskonservative Isolationisten aus den USA, Kommunisten und Greenpeace die Menschheit denn retten?

_Miersch: Vor dem "bösen" freien Markt. Hätten sie Erfolg, wäre dies ein sicheres Rezept für Armut und Rückschritt. Die Länder, die sich im vergangenen Vierteljahrhundert dem Weltmarkt geöffnet haben, wurden dadurch wohlhabender. Und zwar nicht nur die Reichen dort, sondern die Bevölkerungsmehrheit, wie sich an den Statistiken über Lebenserwartung und Kindersterblichkeit ablesen lässt. Die, die sich nach den Rezepten der Globalisierungsgegner abschotteten, verharrten in Armut. Der Unterschied zwischen einer Wirtschaft, die die Chancen der Globalisierung nutzt, und einer, die dies nicht tut, ist einfach zu beschreiben: Es ist der Unterschied zwischen Süd- und Nordkorea. Übrigens: Ökonomische Unfreiheit geht fast immer mit politischer Unterdrückung Hand in Hand. Reiche Diktaturen sind seltene Ausnahmen.

Wie viel Globalisierung ist zu viel?

_Miersch: Nicht zu viel, sondern zu wenig Globalisierung ist das Problem. Denn entgegen allem Globalisierungsgerede wird den Armen die Teilnahme an der Weltwirtschaft durch Einfuhrbeschränkungen und Zölle äußerst schwer gemacht. Die Durchschnittszölle liegen in den reichen Industriestaaten bei zirka 6,3 Prozent. Typische Produkte aus Entwicklungsländern, wie Textilien und Schuhe, werden jedoch mit Zöllen zwischen 15 und 30 Prozent belegt. Manche landwirtschaftlichen Erzeugnisse sogar mit bis zu 550 Prozent. Doch gerade die ärmsten Länder haben nichts anderes als Agrarprodukte zu exportieren. Das Prinzip des Freihandels muss endlich auch dann gelten, wenn der internationale Wettbewerb zu Ungunsten der EU ausfällt.

Kann man hier von Doppelmoral sprechen?

_Miersch: Solidarität mit der Dritten Welt kann heute nur eines heißen: Fairplay, wenn die globale Konkurrenz durch die nachrückenden Länder zunimmt. Aber genau dazu sind viele Globalisierungsgegner nicht bereit. Eine Weihnachtsspende für den armen Kaffeepflücker in Nicaragua? Aber gern. Wehe jedoch, wenn seine Tochter nicht mehr Kaffee pflücken möchte und sie es zur Softwareentwicklerin schafft! Wenn plötzlich billige und gute Computer, Textilien oder Autos auf die europäischen Märkte drängen – aus Ländern, die vorher jahrzehntelang in der Rolle des willigen Abnehmers europäischer Waren gefangen waren – dann ist es schnell vorbei mit der "internationalen Solidarität". Dann protestieren die Bosse der Altindustrien mit den Gewerkschaftern Arm in Arm: Brot für die Welt – aber die Wurst bleibt hier!

Was sagen Sie zu Naomi Kleins Buch "No Logo"?
_Miersch: Ihre Intention mag ja ehrenwert sein. Es ist völlig richtig, Konzernen auf die Finger zu sehen und nachzufragen, wie die Arbeitsbedingungen in ihren Filialen im Ausland sind. Naomi Klein sieht die niedrigen Löhne der Menschen in Asien, Lateinamerika und Afrika und ist empört. Sie hätte jedoch ein wenig genauer hinschauen sollen. Die Alternative zu den Niedriglöhnen heißt nicht Löhne wie in Kanada oder Deutschland. Man kann nicht ohne Übergang von der Agrargesellschaft in den industriellen Wohlfahrtsstaat springen. Die reale Alternative zur Arbeit in Textilfabriken bedeutet, wie die Eltern und Großeltern zu wirtschaften. Die haben einen Großteil ihres Lebens hinter einem Ochsenpflug verbracht. Was Frau Klein bei ihrer Kritik gern vergisst, ist, dass die allermeisten westlichen Konzerne deutlich höhere Löhne bezahlen und bessere Sozialleistungen anbieten als die jeweiligen lokalen Unternehmen. Es bleibt ja nicht bei den Niedriglöhnen. Zwischen 1965 und 1995 stieg das durchschnittliche Pro-Kopf-Einkommen in Südkorea Jahr für Jahr um 7,2 Prozent, in Taiwan um 6,2 Prozent (von solchen Lohnzuwächsen können deutsche Gewerkschafter nur träumen). In Vietnam und Bangladesch wird es ähnlich verlaufen. Ich habe letztens mal einen treffenden Cartoon gesehen, da kriecht ein bettelndes Kind auf einen Globalisierungsgegner zu. Und der sagt zu dem Kind: "Wir helfen dir! Als erstes schließen wir die Turnschuhfabrik in deinem Dorf."

"Manitu trinkt Coca-Cola, großes Indianer-Ehrenwort" – überall, wo wir hinschauen, sehen wir Ikea, Coca-Cola und Philip Morris – was Kritiker als die bunte Welt des Kulturimperialismus bezeichnen. Eine Ära des "Brand-Brain-Washing"? Würden Sie, Herr Maxeiner, wenn Sie könnten, Deutschland zur McDonald's-freien Zone erklären und so wie die Franzosen Englisch aus unserem Wortschatz verbannen?

_Maxeiner: Bloß nicht. Siehe oben, Pax Big Mac. Wir haben keine Lust auf ökologisch korrekte Volksküche nach dem Vorbild des nationalsozialistischen Eintopf-Sonntags. Als wir hörten, dass Bundestagspräsident Thierse gesetzlich vorgeschriebene Quoten für deutsche Musik fordert, glaubten wir erst an einen Scherz. Aber der meint das ernst. Das ist der Geist gescheiterter Volkserzieher.

Luxussteuer, Alkoholsteuer, Mineralölsteuer, Tabaksteuer, Pfand auf Dosen, was kommt als Nächstes, die Luftsteuer?
_Maxeiner: Die ist schon da. Jeder Mensch atmet Kohlendioxid aus. Und Kohlendioxid heizt angeblich das Klima auf. 4.000 deutsche Fabriken bekommen deshalb demnächst vom Staat Kohlendioxidquoten zugeteilt. Wer mehr ausstößt, muss Zertifikate hinzukaufen. Zum erstenmal in der Menschheitsgeschichte wird mit heißer Luft gehandelt. /////

[1] Das Mephisto-Prinzip: Warum es besser ist, nicht gut zu sein. [www.eichborn.de]

[2] Adam Smith, 1723-1790, war ein bedeutender schottischer Philosoph und für sein wegweisendes Buch über Freihandel und Marktökonomie, "The Wealth of Nations", bekannter Ökonom. Quelle: Enzyklopädie Brockhaus. [www.brockhaus.de]

[3] www.heritage.org

Michael Miersch
Geboren 1956 in Frankfurt am Main, volontierte bei der "taz" und war Redakteur der Umweltmagazine "Chancen" und "Natur". Seit 1993 schreibt er als selbständiger Publizist für große Zeitungen, Zeitschriften und Radiosender im deutschsprachigen Raum. Darüber hinaus ist Miersch Autor zahlreicher Sachbücher und Dokumentarfilme, wofür er zahlreiche Auszeichnungen in den USA und Deutschland erhalten hat.

Dirk Maxeiner
Geboren 1953, war Redakteur beim "Stern" und entwickelte in den achtziger Jahren in Paris das Stadtmagazin "Pariser Luft". Er war dort Chefredakteur und Herausgeber. Danach zeichnete er für Idee und Entwicklung des Umweltmagazins "Chancen" verantwortlich, wo er Chefredakteur bis 1988 war. Anschließend war er bis 1993 Chefredakteur der Zeitschrift "Natur", der zu dieser Zeit größten europäischen Umweltzeitschrift. Seit 1993 arbeitet Maxeiner als Publizist.

Die Zukunft und ihre Feinde, Maxeiner/Miersch, Eichborn
Das Mephisto-Prinzip, Maxeiner/Miersch, Eichborn
Lexikon der Öko-Irrtümer, Maxeiner/Miersch, Eichborn

www.maxeiner-miersch.de
www.eichborn.de

Selected Advertisements
· SELECTED ADS ·
· SELECTED ADS ·
· SELECTED ADS ·
· SELECTED ADS

DER NEUE HERRENDUFT
YVES SAINT LAURENT
M7

hillside su hotel **antalya** turkey
only 60 meters to the pool bar

LIVE FROM LONDON
BURBERRY
BRIT
A NEW FRAGRANCE FOR WOMEN

CHANEL
J12
AUTOMATIC
SWISS MADE
J 12
DIAMANTS

CHANEL
CHANEL
J12
AUTOMATIC
SWISS
MADE
J 12
DIAMANTS
LISTE DER AUTHORISIERTEN VERKAUFSSTELLEN UNTER: 01801 - 24 26 35 (ORTSTARIF)
www.chanel.com

Cuiron photographed by Irving Penn in New York, N.Y. - 2002

HELMUT LANG
est.1986
CUIRON
POUR HOMME
EAU DE COLOGNE
3.3 Fl. Oz.
NEW YORK

Selected Advertisements

A selection of advertisements chosen exclusively by M on the criteria of a superb visual concept and an excellent communication scheme. For further details, see below.

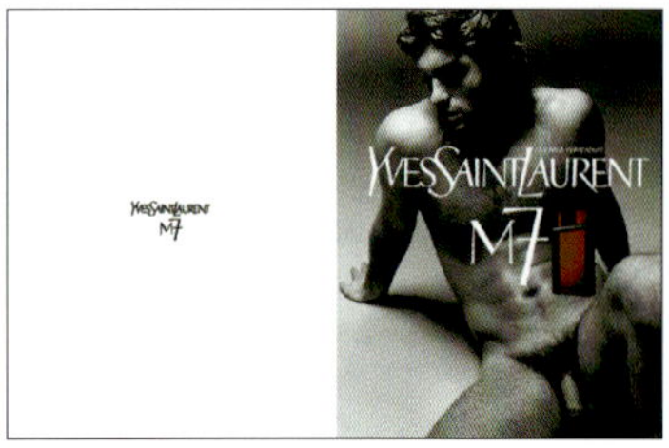

01. YVES SAINT LAURENT

02. DESIGN HOTELS

03. BURBERRY

04. CHANEL

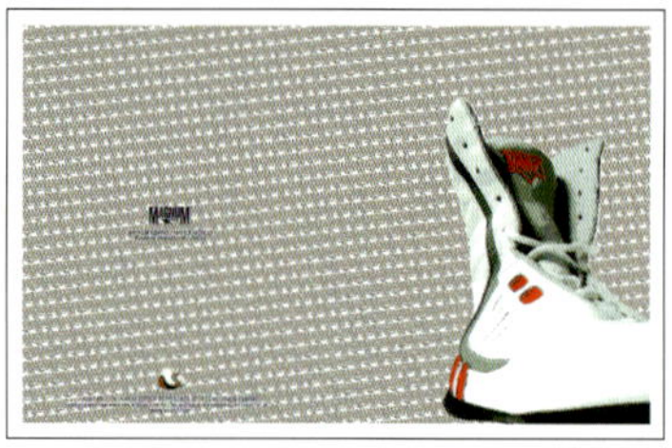

05. MAGNUM

06. HELMUT LANG

| 01. YVES SAINT LAURENT | Agency: In-House. CD: Tom Ford. Photography: Solve Sundsbo. Styling: Simon Costin. Make Up: Marla Olsson. Hair: Sam McKnight. www.ysl-m7.com | 02. DESIGN HOTELS | Agency: Lebensart Global Networks AG. CD: Claus Sendlinger. Photography: Tamer Yilmaz. AD & Design: Michael Schickinger. Copywriter: Scott Crouch. www.designhotels.com | 03. BURBERRY | Agency: In-House. CD: Fabien Baron. Photography: Mario Testino. Model: Ben Grimes. Product Shot: Raymond Meier. www.burberry.com | 04. CHANEL | Agency: In-House. CD: Jacque Hellau. www.chanel.com | 05 MAGNUM | Agency: M-109 Network. CD: Piero Borsellino, Kimberly Lloyd. Styling: Kills.de. www.hi-tec.com | 06. HELMUT LANG | Agency: In-House. CD: Irving Penn, Helmut Lang. Photography: Irving Penn. Styling: Phyllis Posnick. AD: Baron & Baron, Stephen Wong. Design: Stephen Wong. www.helmutlang.com

If your advertisement is suitable for the next volumes "surprise" or "tomorrow", contact: Media@M-Publication.com

Vote&Win. What's your favourite ad? TDK XS-IV80 Multimedia Speaker System

WinTDK@M-Publication.com. Closing Date: 30.11.2003. The course of law is excluded.

Catching l'air du temps

Sarah of Colette, the owner of a four-storey shop in the heart of Paris, on extravagant advertisements and artificial shortages of luxury items.

Colette, a girl's name, a boutique, a design store, a gallery, a party? What is the "Colette"?
_Colette is all this: A "lieu de rencontres", a meeting place for people and the media – fashion, design, art, food, music, beauty and other pleasures. Colette first opened on the 21st of March 1997. Since then, I always wanted to create a store which is like a magazine, with pages for art, for fashion, etc. Colette is an inspirational source to touch all the senses.

Colette features a diversity of products from "Andrée Putman Perfume" to a "Lomo Supersampler". What are the criteria for the products that you choose?
_Quality and the originality count. It is not only the surface of the product but also the inside and where the product comes from. You may see the surface at first glance, but later you will find out about the inside. I do not want to disappoint my customers. So I take a closer look down to the last detail.

Is Colette the place for the rich and the affluent cosmopolitan jet-setters of our society? Or is it more a place to indulge in luxury but nevertheless find some articles for a smaller budget?
_We have a huge diversity of customers of all ages, from all countries, and with different spending budgets. For their varying needs, we offer a variety of products at all prices. We like this mix of luxurious to affordable goods, that are nonetheless extremely original.

Fragrances are mostly designed to look expensive and extravagant. Millions of dollars are spent on designing the bottle, the packaging and, of course, advertising campaigns. Other brands such as "Kiehl's" known for its tradition or "Holi-Eau" from the little spa in Nice are on the contrary more minimalist and less decorative in their design. What is behind this?
_Mainstream consumers understand the surface of the product as an indicator for quality and tradition, which is why major brands exaggerate sometimes. Others pay much more attention to the product. While shaping and designing the product, the budget goes into the product itself, its ingredients and its quality. The effectiveness takes priority.

How would you define luxury for the 21st century?
_Luxury is a personal thing. Everyone defines it for themselves. Luxury is a point of view and a matter of having options. At Colette, you have the choice between a vast variety of products from international places, while geographically you are still in Paris.

Is the price tag an indicator for something extremely valuable and at the same time a must for style junkies?
_Again, we have all kind of prices. The style junkie decides for themselves whether they want product A or product B. It is not the price tag that indicates value but the option that a person has at Colette.

Why is visual art and music essential for your concept?
_Magazines and other print publications are as important as fashion, beauty, etc. Music is "today", and we always try to catch "l'air du temps".

Is Colette a kind of a style guidance for its visitors?
_Maybe, why not? We offer a selection of products, of "trends", but we leave the visitor free to take them as inspiration on their own way. Style is not about the brand's name on a garment, but the way you wear it. The word "style" is magic. So we shouldn't get confused about someone or something being "stylish" or not.

What is the cheapest and the most expensive article?
_The cheapest: Guimauve[1] for one euro. Most expensive: Chrome Hearts-Rolling Stones belt in diamonds.

Which other companies and artists are you collaborating with on special edition products?
_Special Trench Stoty this autumn: 10 designers agreed to redesign seven trench coats exclusively for Colette, in black: Alaia, Lanvin, Burberry, Marc Jacobs, Prada, Haider Ackerman, Yves Saint Laurent Rive Gauche, Comme des Garçons, Jil Sander, Dior Homme. A new CD, House of Colette and a new CD Colette No. 6, exhibitions by Joseph Szabo and Michael Bevilacqua.

What is the secret of limiting products?
_You said it: to be limited. /////

[1] Guimauve, french word for marshmallow, a very soft light sweet that is white or pink. [www.Langenscheidt.de]

Colette, 213 rue Saint-Honoré, F-75001 Paris
T. +33.1 55 35 33 90, www.colette.fr

Selected Advertisements

Luxury is a matter of point of view

_Man versehe mich mit Luxus. Auf alles Notwendige kann ich verzichten. *Oscar Wilde, Schriftsteller (1854-1900)*
_Luxury is a beer, a cigarette, and writing that perfect track on a summer's day. *Blaine Arnold, musician, 27*
_Luxus ist immer relativ. *Michael Miersch, Pubilizist, 47*
_One must be poor to know the luxury of giving. *George Eliot, author (1819 - 1880)*
_Luxury for me personally would mean perfect functionality and efficiency. *Dov Charney, industrialist, 34*
_Ich wünsche mir noch ein Barbie and ein Barbie Haus. *Michelle, Schülerin, 7*
_Luxus ist das, was man sich nicht leisten kann, und das, was man gerade nicht besitzt. *Ardi Goldman, Bauherr, 40*
_Luxury is the ability to transform yourself. *Rilla Alexander, designer, 28*
_Ficken ohne Gummi. *Felix Schwenzel, Autor, 34*
_Morgens mal ausschlafen zu können. Das wäre im Moment Luxus für mich. *Christina, Mutter, 26*
_Vacation used to be a luxury, however, in today's world, it has become a necessity. *unknown*
_War has become a luxury that only small nations can afford. *Hannah Arendt, author, (1906 - 1975)*
_Viel mehr Burger King Filialen. *Florian, Student, 24*
_Zum Fussball ziehe ich mir meine Nikes an. Damit bin ich schneller als die anderen. *Luca, 7*
_Luxury is having more spare time. *Johan Norberg, Author, 30*
_Luxus muß sein. Wenn die Reichen nichts verschwenden, verhungern die Armen.
Charles de Montesquieu, Staatstheoretiker (1689-1755)

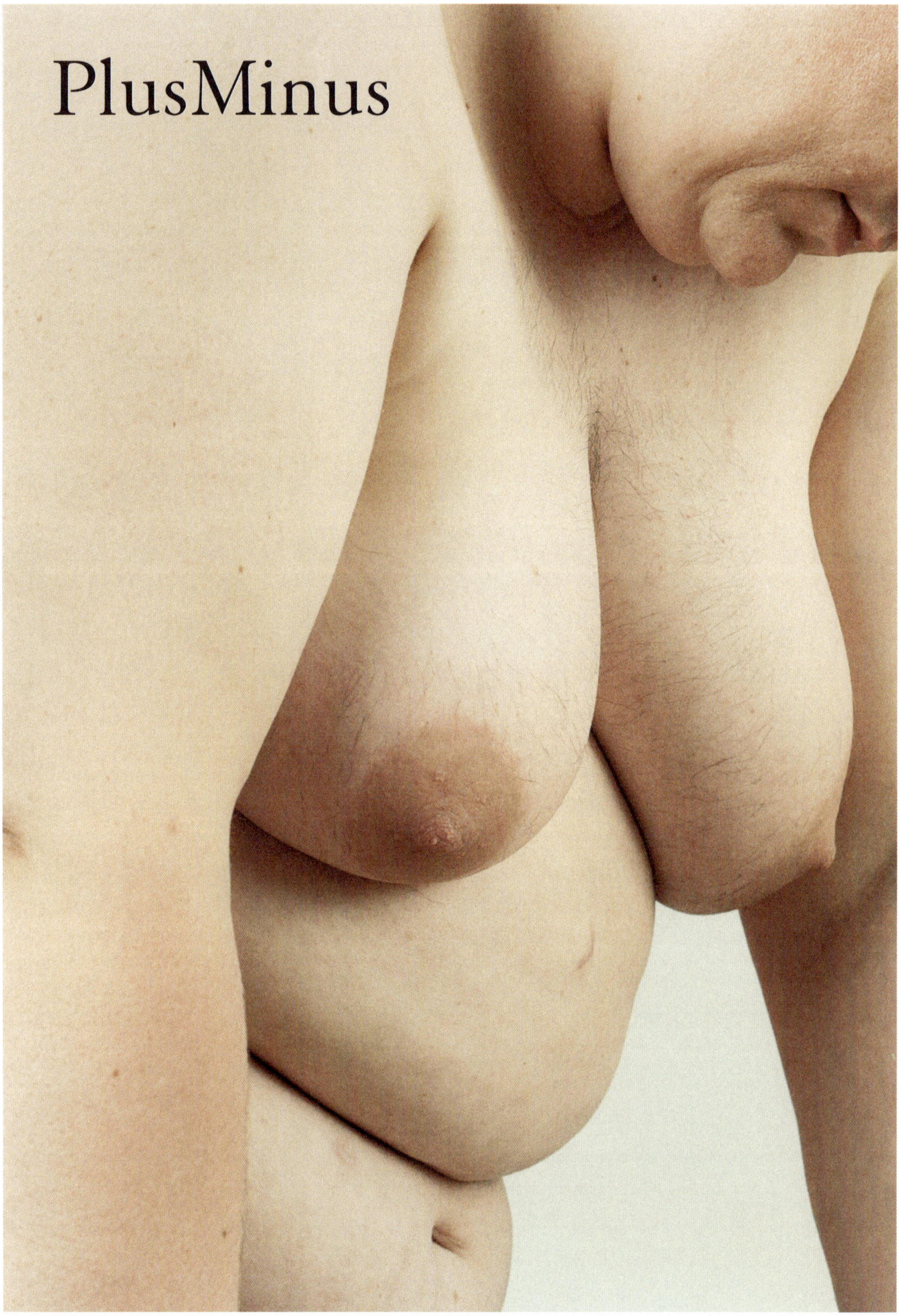

PHOTOGRAPHY BY
SABINE SCHRÜNDER _FOTO-UNION.DE

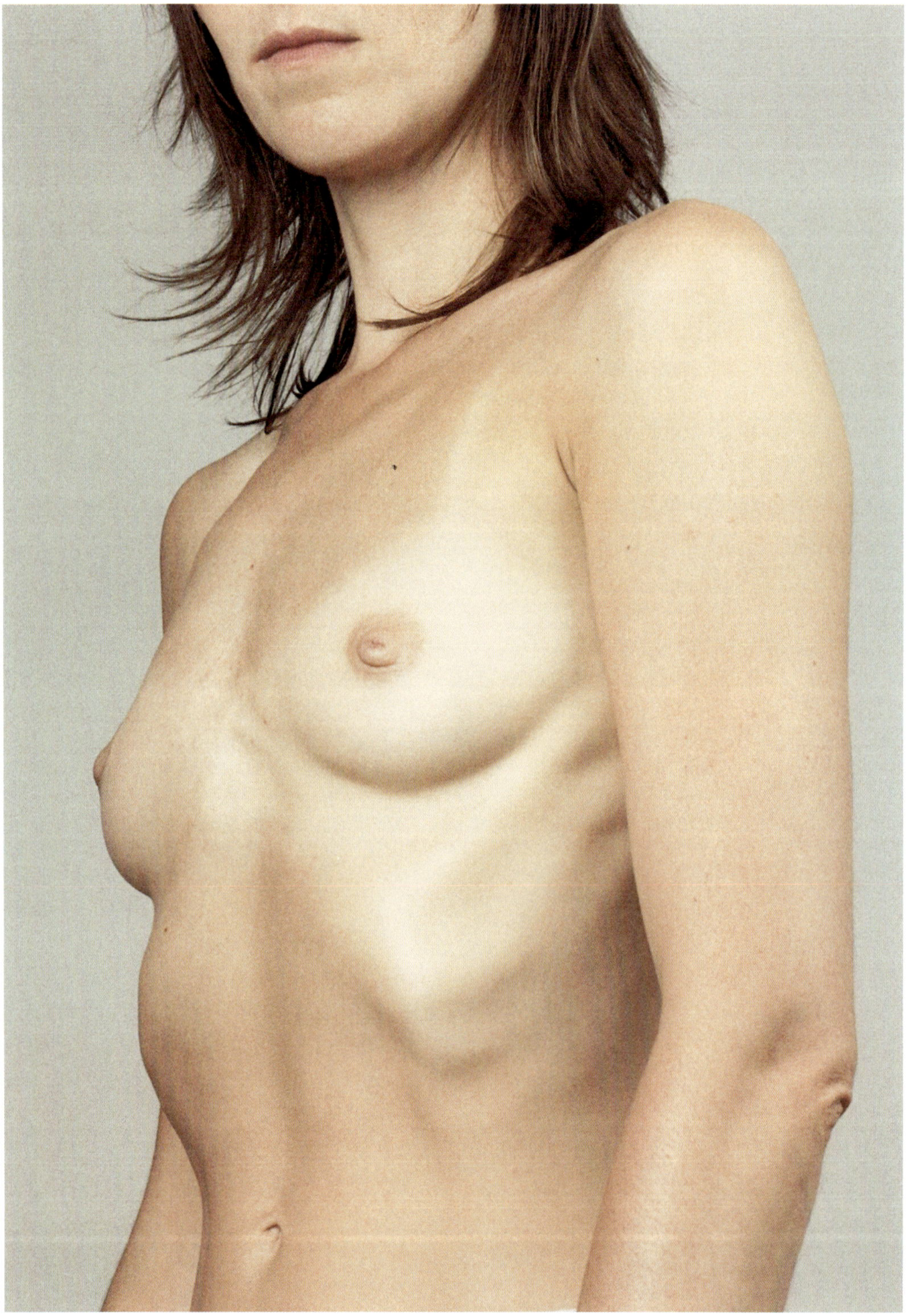

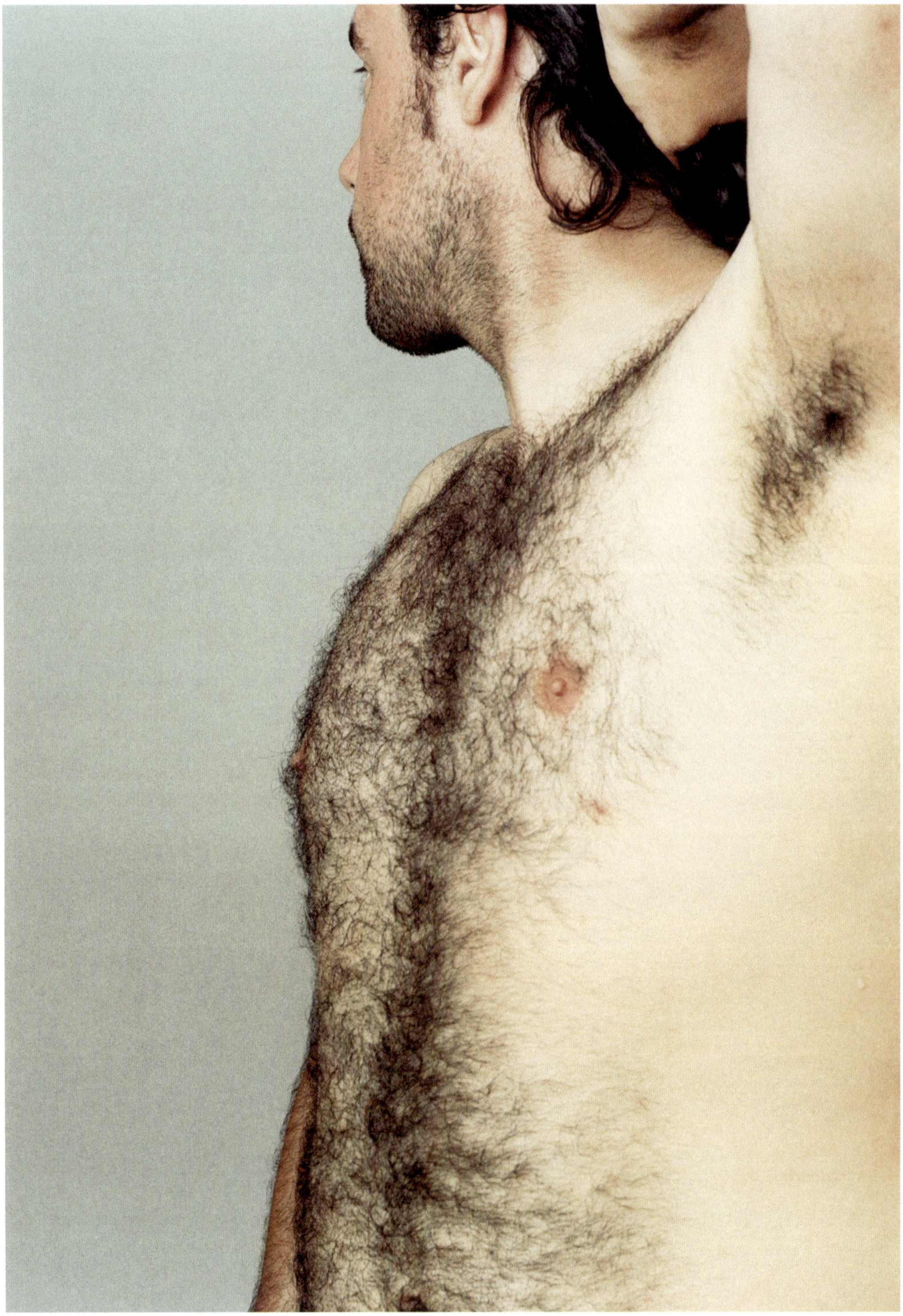

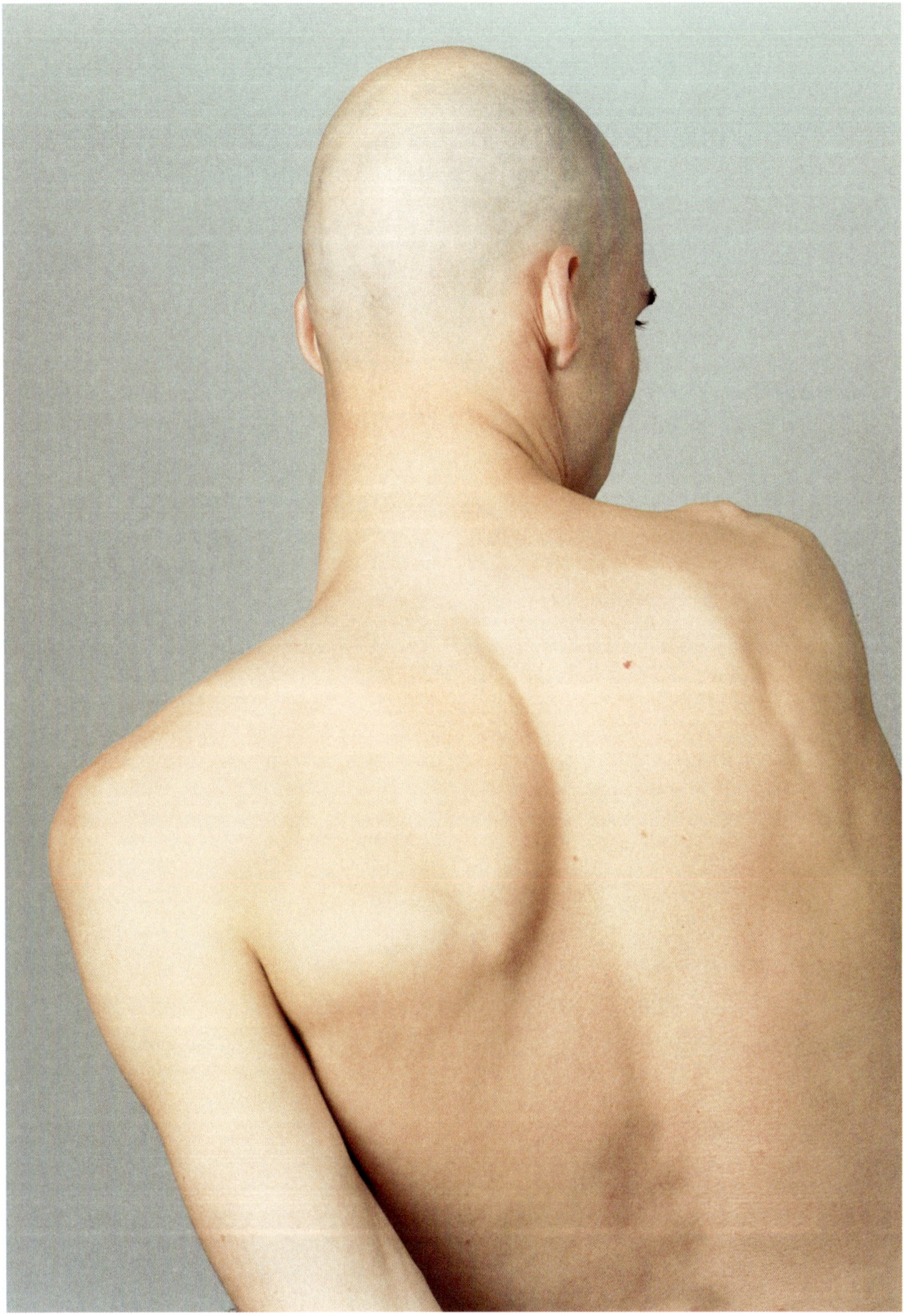

BY KIMBERLY LLOYD

Men who apologise for being rich will not remain rich for long

The redistribution of wealth from the producers to those who have done nothing for it requires only envy and the pointing of a gun – whether by a robber armed with a weapon or a legislator armed with a bill. Ayn Rand, the author of "Atlas Shrugged" on the production of wealth, independent effort and her homage to those who create and created value in today's society.

Miss Rand, what is money?
_Money rests on the axiom that every man is the owner of his mind and his effort.

Money is not simply seen as a medium of exchange in financial transactions, but also in an evil light. Why is that?
_Run for your life from any man who tells you that money is evil. That sentence is the leper's bell of an approaching looter. So long as men live together on earth and need means to deal with one another – their only substitute, if they abandon money, is the muzzle of a gun. Money is a tool of exchange, which can't exist unless there are goods produced and men able to produce them. Money is the material shape of the principle that men who wish to deal with one another must deal by trade and give value for value. Money is not the tool of the moochers, who claim your product by tears, or of the looters, who take it from you by force. Money is made possible only by the men who produce. Try to grow a seed of wheat without the knowledge left to you by men who had to discover it for the first time. Try to obtain your food by means of nothing but physical motions – and you'll learn that man's mind is the root of all the goods produced and of all the wealth that has ever existed on earth. Is this what you consider evil?

But why does the most quoted verse in the Bible, Timothy II, 6:10, say, "The love of money is the root of all evil"?
_To love a thing is to know and love its nature. To love money is to know and love the fact that money is the creation of the best power within you, and your passkey to trade your effort for the effort of the best among men. It's the person who would sell his soul for a nickel, who is the loudest in proclaiming his hatred of money – and he has good reason to hate it. The lovers of money are willing to work for it. They know they are able to deserve it. Let me give you a tip on a clue to men's characters: the man who damns money has obtained it dishonorably; the man who respects it has earned it.

We face the perverse injustice of making scapegoats out of businessmen. Some people even say that money is produced by the strong at the expense of the weak?
_What strength do you mean? It is not the strength of guns or muscles. Wealth is the product of man's capacity to think. Then is money made by the man who invents a motor at the expense of those who did not invent it? Is money made by the intelligent at the expense of the fools? By the able at the expense of the incompetent? By the ambitious at the expense of the lazy? Money is made – before it can be looted or mooched – made by the effort of every honest man, each to the extent of his ability.

What is an honest man in this context?
_An honest man is one who knows that he can't consume more than he has produced.

The affluent sometimes feel ashamed and guilty for their properties.
_Men who have no courage, pride, or self-esteem, men who have no moral sense of their right to their money and are not willing to defend it as they defend their life, men who apologize for being rich – will not remain rich for long.

Infectious greed is to blame for the scandals engulfing companies. But private men are just as eager to lie, cheat and steal in pursuit of profit, making crooks and criminals out of themselves.
_If the source is corrupt, you have damned your own existence. Did you get your money by fraud? By pandering to men's vices or men's stupidity? By catering to fools, in the hope of getting more than your ability deserves? By lowering your standards? By doing work you despise for purchasers you scorn? If so, then your money will not give you a moment's or a penny's worth of joy. Then all the things you buy will become, not a tribute to you, but a reproach; not an achievement, but a reminder of shame.

Can one buy happiness?

_Money will not purchase happiness for the man who has no concept of what he wants; money will not give him a code of values, if he's evaded the knowledge of what to value, and it will not provide him with a purpose, if he's evaded the choice of what to seek. Money will not buy intelligence for the fool, or admiration for the coward, or respect for the incompetent. It will take you wherever you wish, but it will not replace you as the driver. Money is the product of virtue, but it will not give you virtue and it will not redeem your vices. Money will not give you the unearned, neither in matter nor in spirit. It will give you the means for the satisfaction of your desires, but it will not provide you with desires.

Does an heir deserve his fortune even if he has not actively produced it?

_Only the man who does not need it, is fit to inherit wealth – the man who would make his own fortune no matter where he started. If an heir is equal to his money, it serves him; if not, it destroys him.

What is the difference between America and other wealthy nations?

_If you ask me to name the proudest distinction of Americans, I would choose – because it contains all the others – the fact that they were the people who created the phrase "to make money". No other language or nation had ever used these words before; men had always thought of wealth as a static quantity – to be seized, begged, inherited, shared, looted, or obtained as a favor. Americans were the first to understand that wealth has to be created. The words "to make money" hold the essence of human morality.

Americans invented the term "making money" but who is the real maker of wealth?

_To the glory of mankind, there was, for the first and only time in history, a country of money – and I have no higher, more reverent tribute to pay to America, for this means: a country of reason, justice, freedom, production, achievement. For the first time, man's mind and money were set free, and there were no fortunes-by-conquest, but only fortunes-by-work, and instead of swordsmen and slaves, there appeared the real maker of wealth, the greatest worker, the highest type of human being – the self-made man – the American industrialist. /////

Ayn Rand [1905-1982]
Rand was born in St Petersburg, Russia, on 2 February 1905. Rand graduated from the University of Petrograd, receiving her diploma in philosophy and history. In 1926, she arrived in New York City and after six months she left for Hollywood to pursue a career as a screenwriter. She began writing The Fountainhead in 1935, which was initially rejected by twelve publishers. But when it finally got printed in 1943, it made history by becoming a best-seller. In 1951, she devoted herself completely to "Atlas Shrugged", Rand's Magnum Opus. In this novel she dramatised her unique philosophy in an intellectual mystery story that integrated ethics, metaphysics, epistemology, politics, economics and sex. Although she considered herself to be primarily a fiction writer, she realised that in order to create heroic fictional characters, she had to identify the philosophic principles which make such individuals possible. She needed to formulate "a philosophy for living on earth". Thereafter, Ayn Rand wrote and lectured on her philosophy – objectivism. She published and edited her own periodicals from 1962 to 1976, her essays providing much of the material for nine books on objectivism and its application to culture. Ayn Rand died on 6 March 1982, in her New York City apartment. Her vision of man and her philosophy for living on earth have changed the lives of thousands of readers and launched a philosophic movement with a growing impact on American culture.

Interview
The above interview is fictional, based on the "Money Speech" of Francisco d'Anconia, copper industrialist, heir to an enormous fortune. It is said that the main characters of the novel "Atlas Shrugged" represent Rand's philosophy of "Objectivism".

Sources
Miss Rand's answers are quotations from "Atlas Shrugged", pages 382 to 386 and "For the new intellectual", pages 88 to 94. Both books are published by Signet – Penguin Group.

⇛ www.aynrand.de

Money is the sixth sense, and you
can't make use of the other five without it.

William Somerset Maugham

1874-1965, British novelist, playwright, short-story writer,
highest paid author in the world in the 1930s.

FEDERAL RESERVE NOTE
THE UNITED STATES OF AMERICA
D 99824002 A
WASHINGTON, D.C.
THIS NOTE IS LEGAL TENDER
FOR ALL DEBTS, PUBLIC AND PRIVATE
4
A4
4
D

Lee

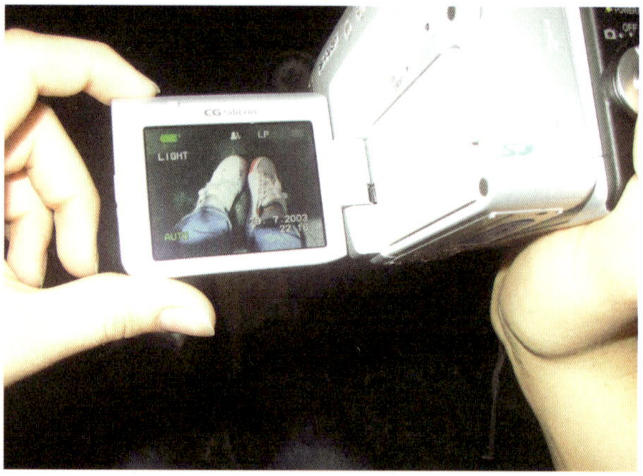
LIGHT
AUTO

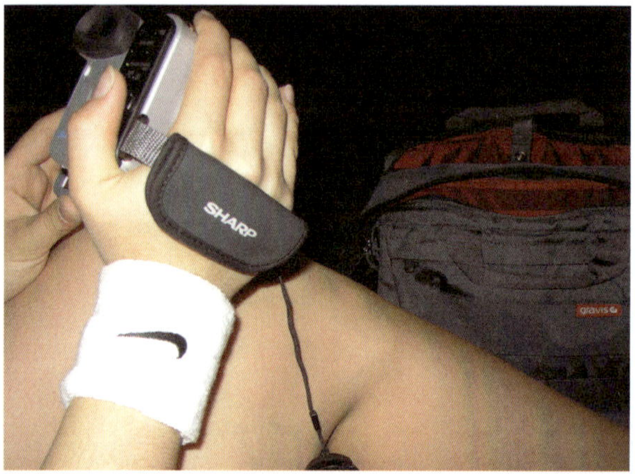
SHARP

IMAGES SHOT ON _SHARP VIEWCAM VL-Z5S. _WWW.SHARP.COM. MODEL _VANESSA. CLOTHES _LEE AUTUMN/WINTER 2003.
SHOES _GRAVIS TARMAC. _BYRON. BAG _GRAVIS DIGIBAG CHARCOAL. _MACY LAVENDER.
GOGGLES _SPEEDO. GAME _SCRABBLE MAGNETICS. TECHNICAL ACCESSORIES _SHARP MINI-DISC-RECORDER DR470H.

The creative director was unable to find the appropriate script for this photo essay. M is desperately in search of a story.

PHOTOGRAPHY BY
KIMBERLY LLOYD

Respond&Win. Write a story.
Gravis Footwear and Gravis Digibags.

WinGravis@M-Publication.com. Closing date: 30.11.2003. The course of law is excluded.

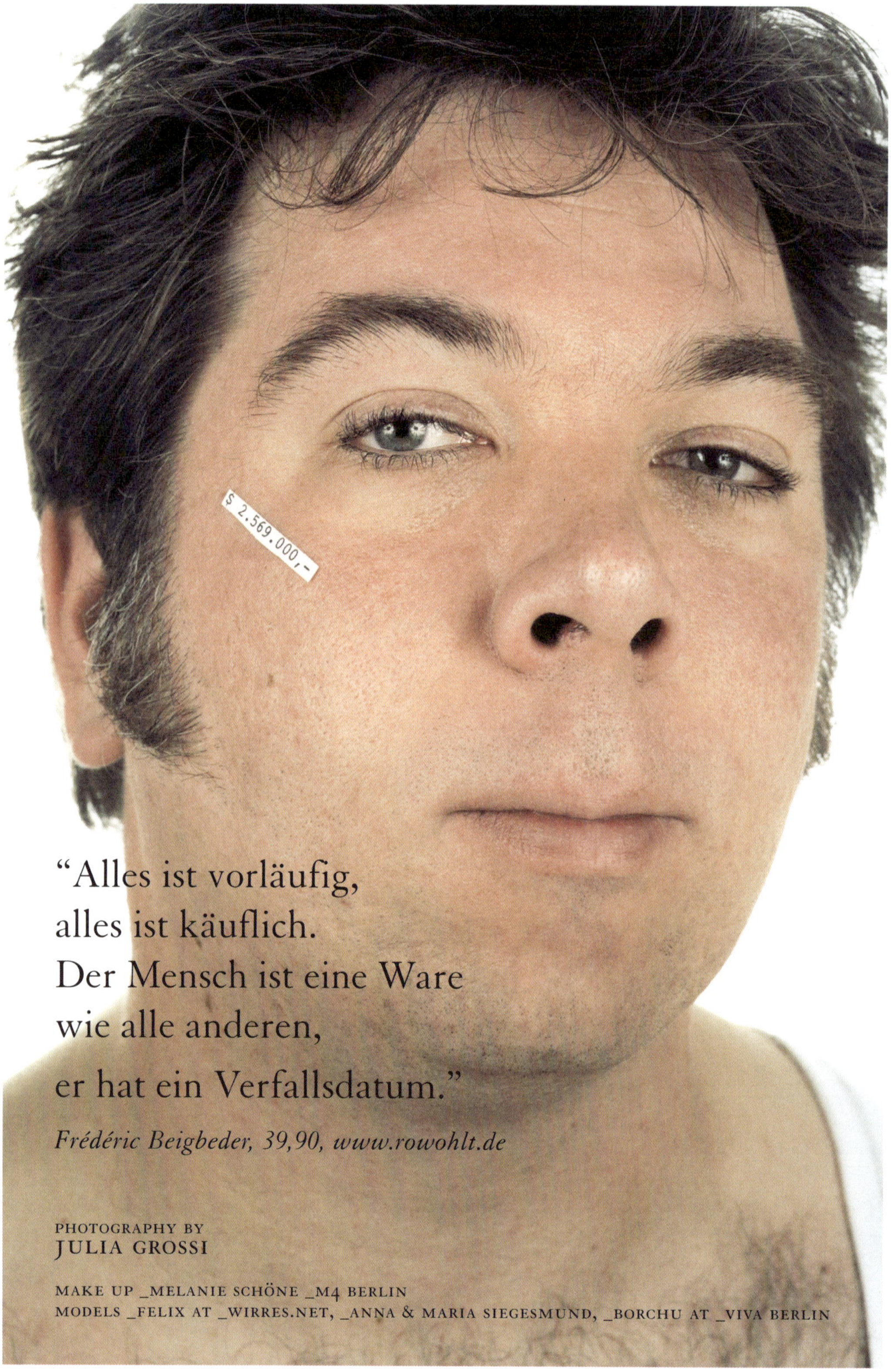

$ 2.569.000,-
"Alles ist vorläufig,
alles ist käuflich.
Der Mensch ist eine Ware
wie alle anderen,
er hat ein Verfallsdatum."
Frédéric Beigbeder, 39,90, www.rowohlt.de
PHOTOGRAPHY BY
JULIA GROSSI
MAKE UP _MELANIE SCHÖNE _M4 BERLIN
MODELS _FELIX AT _WIRRES.NET, _ANNA & MARIA SIEGESMUND, _BORCHU AT _VIVA BERLIN

FELIX IS SHAVED WITH
KIEHL'S CLOSE-SHAVERS SQUADRON FORMULA 31

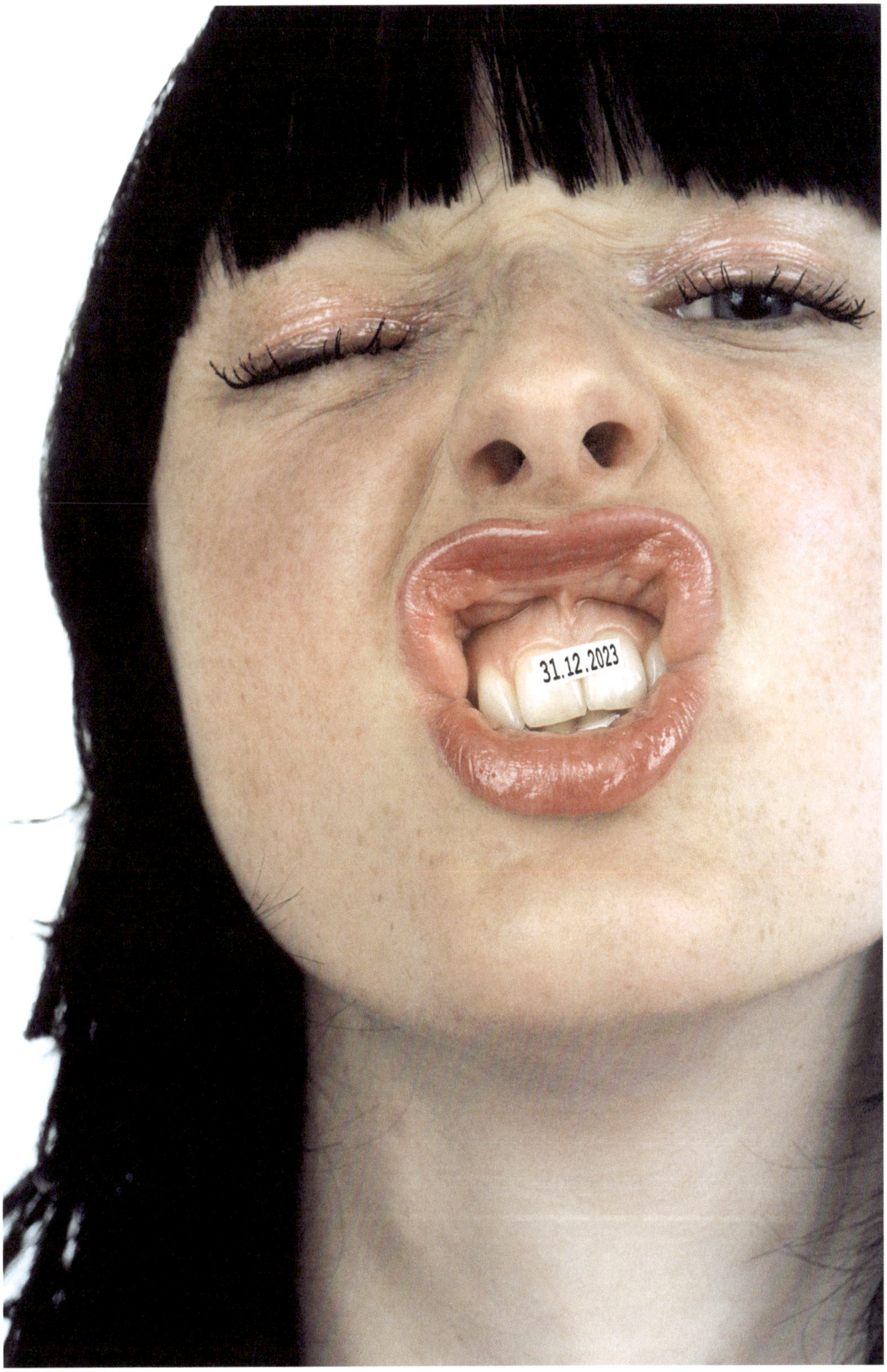

MARIA WEARS KIEHL'S LIP PAINT PINK PEARL,
YSL LIPMARKER PINK, YSL TEINT TEINT ÉCLAT DE SOIE FOR FOUNDATION

ANNA WEARS KIEHL'S LIP GLOSS PINK PEARL, YSL TEINT PARFAIT, YSL OMBRE SOLO 10 AND YSL OMBRE SOLO 3 FOR THE EYES, YSL BLUSH VARIATION FOR THE CHEEKS

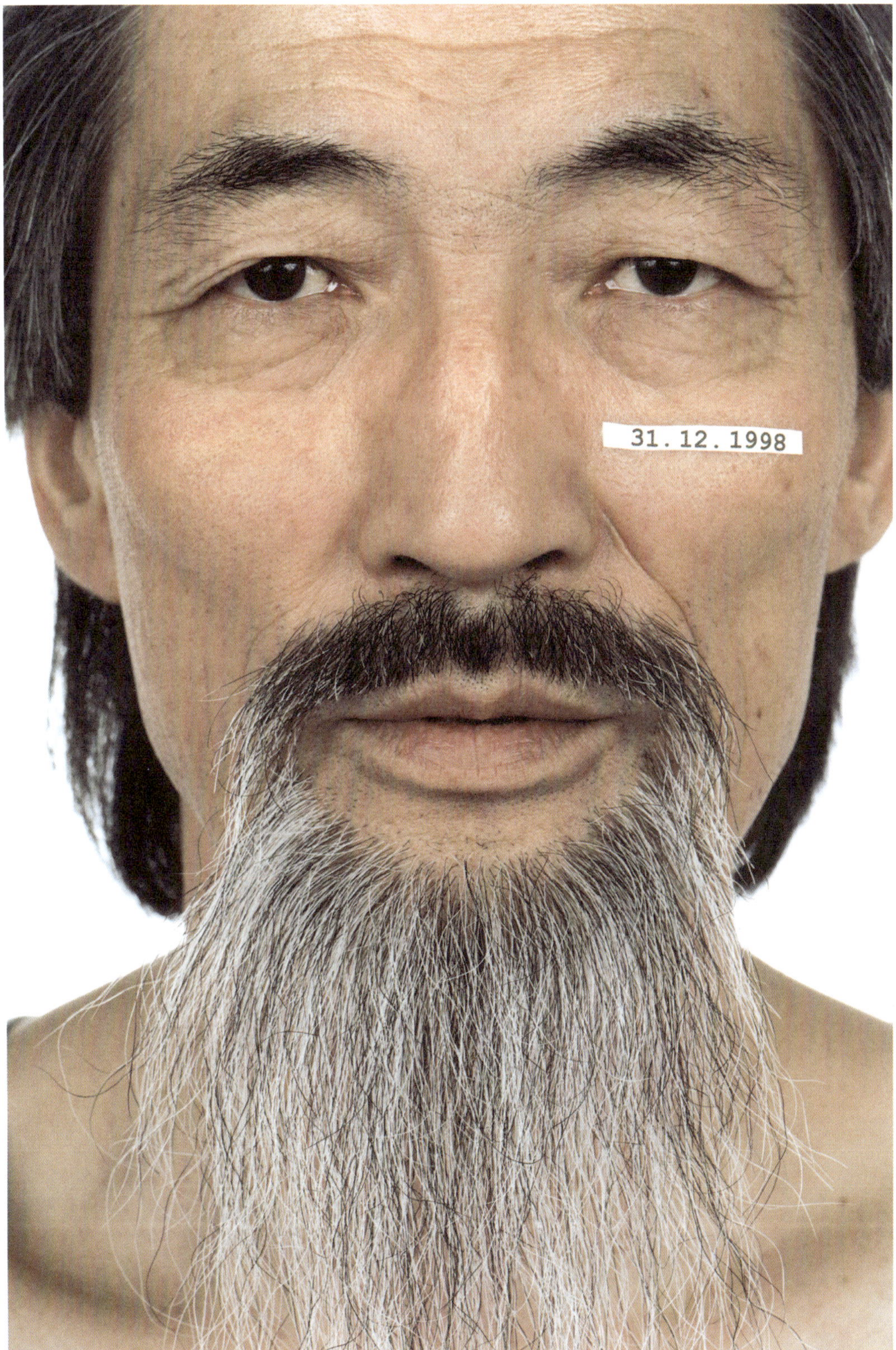

BORCHU WEARS CHANEL POUDRE UNIVERSELLE LIBRE – CLAIR TRANSLUCENT.
HAIR FINISHED WITH KIEHL'S HAIR CONDITIONER AND GROOMING AID FORMULA 133

Window reflections

PHOTOGRAPHY BY
LEILA MENDEZ

WORDS BY
ANDREAS BAIER

The unbeatable advantage of youth is classless thinking. As long as certain attitudes or mental correction by your parents did not influence you, you will have basically selected your friends and social surroundings by yourself or in line with the opinions of other friends you looked up to. One so-called attitude is the way you dress, depending on whether you had been able to enjoy the luxurious advantage of being allowed to create your own outfit – or not. Boys normally prefer practical clothing. They do not care about adjectives like pretty, smart, cute or whatever as long as they can play football without being brought to justice by a headache-suffering mother afterwards. Girls, however, are differently structured. They wear a badge on their foreheads, displaying Barbie chip inside, which keeps them constantly in front of any mirror that they can occupy, even if it is a mirrored shop window.

So what makes parents present their children like this? In some ways, kids might be nothing but toys they love to play with. Like a car, a house, a horse, a dog, diamonds

or a healthy bank account. All of these items represent social standing, but they also mean the owners accept certain rules that keep our society functional. They see it as their duty to honour these laws by introducing their up-and-coming family members with precisely these mechanisms. To me, special family events, such as First Communion, birthday parties, Christmas or similar happenings, were directly linked to wearing clothes I did not like at all. I always found myself looking awfully stupid and – even worse – the wool was unacceptably scratching my skin! I felt quite uncomfortable and there was not a single argument that could have made the vision of becoming an adult look appealing to me. So here we are. Wearing pretty clothes is not only a question of celebrating superficiality. It is also a matter of training the youth to deal with unusual or unpleasant situations and to stand their own ground, man or woman. Conclusion: whenever we see completely overdressed people worshipping the Holy Lord of surface, we shall never ever underestimate the educational aspect of looking good!

You look, you steal.

Unermüdlich streiten sich angebliche Urheber über die Exklusivität ihrer Gedanken und sprechen von Diebstahl des geistigen Eigentums. Wir sprachen mit Rechtsanwalt Jens Olaf Brelle über Ideenklau.

Juristisch gesehen: Was ist überhaupt eine Idee?
_Ideen sind Entwürfe, Visionen, Vorhaben, Möglichkeiten, Veränderungen, Gedanken, Potentiale, Träume, Schöpfungen, Kreationen, Baupläne und Muster. Vorbilder, die Ziele, Werte, Energie, Fakten, Wissen, Anweisungen, Konzepte, Informationen beinhalten und die zukunftsweisend, kraftvoll, transformierend, umwelt- und umstandsbezogen, verantwortungsvoll und vorausschauend sein sollten.

Und philosophisch?
_Eine Idee ist eine 'mentale Repräsentation', die abstrakt und universell ist. Es gibt Philosophen wie Platon, der sich die "Urbilder" der Dinge und Zahlen als Ideen in einer anderen, von der erfahrbaren getrennt existierenden Welt vorstellte (en el mas allá, jenseits), und er versinnbildlichte das im Gleichnis von der Höhle. In diesem Bild bedeutete die Sonne die perfekte, absolute Idee, die vom Guten, von der Wahrheit und Schönheit. Die Ideen, die in dieser anderen Welt "leben", sind die Vorformen, Modelle, Strukturen der Sachen und der Lebewesen unserer Welt.

Das "Gedankengut" wird als geistiges Eigentum angesehen. Wem gehört die Idee?
_Dem "Erfinder", natürlich nur soweit tatsächlich geistiges Eigentum besteht. Müsste man gesondert prüfen.

Ist eine Idee urheberrechtlich schützbar?
_Nein, grundsätzlich nicht. Es herrscht der Grundsatz der Nachahmungsfreiheit. Erst wenn eine Idee eine eigene Gestaltungshöhe erreicht, wird sie zum "Werk" im urheberrechtlichen Sinne und ist damit schützbar. Lediglich technische Erfindungen können auch als Idee im Patentschutz geistigen Eigentumsschutz erlangen.

Ist das vielleicht der Versuch der künstlichen Verknappung? Wird die Idee somit wertvoller gemacht?
_In gewisser Weise ja. Quasi Wertsteigerung durch Verknappung. Hinsichtlich des sonstigen Schutzes vor Ideenklau bleibt nur die Strategie der Geheimhaltung, bis die Idee einen eigenen Werkcharakter erreicht hat und somit Urheberrechtsschutz erhält. Doch auch dann gilt es, "Beweise" zu sichern. Denn am Urheber liegt es in einem möglichen Gerichtsprozess, die Urheberschaft des geistigen Werks zu beweisen.

Um sich die Exklusivität seiner Idee zu sichern, muss man also einen nachprüfbaren Beweis erbringen. Hier zählt letztlich der Zeitpunkt. Kann der Entstehungszeitpunkt einer Idee als Beweisgrundlage gezählt werden?
_Voraussetzung beispielsweise für eine Patentanmeldung ist die Neuheit der Erfindung. Sollen Ideen (technische Erfindungen) Patentschutz erlangen, kann man diese nur durch die Patentanmeldung erreichen. Der Entstehungszeitpunkt einer Idee ist sonst nicht nachweisbar. Hier zählt also Schnelligkeit! Insofern gilt hier in der Tat: "Wer zuerst kommt, mahlt auch zuerst." In urheberrechtlichen Streitigkeiten (hier fehlt es ja an einer formellen Anmeldung) ist gerade diese Frage immer ein häufiger Streitpunkt, da der vermeintliche Nachahmer immer wieder behauptet, er hätte schon vorher die gleiche Idee gehabt. Und das ist schwer zu widerlegen.

In den 80er Jahren stand die Qualität beim Kauf eines Albums im Vordergrund. Doch heute haben wir dieses Problem mit CDs und DVDs nicht mehr. Ist das Copyright im digitalen Zeitalter noch zeitgerecht?
_Es ist wichtiger denn je. Die Musikindustrie hat mittlerweile zur Kenntnis genommen, dass in ein paar Jahren auch kommerzielles Filesharing ein fester Vertriebskanal von Musik sein wird. Das digitale Rechtemanagement setzt geradezu auf dem "Copyright" auf. Dieses ist daher unverzichtbar.

Wenn man sich eine Software kopiert, heißt es nicht mehr Raubkopie, sondern nur noch Kopie. Radiosender und Clubs zahlen keine Gema-Gebühren mehr. Fotos aus dem Internet dürfen für Kampagnen verwendet werden. Ein Exklusivrecht auf einen Namen gibt es auch nicht mehr. Das Ende der Copyfights. Willkommen im "Royalty-free Rights Eldorado"?
_Soweit man da an "Copyleft" oder ähnliche Formen denkt, ist dies wohl in absehbarer Zeit nicht denkbar. Vielmehr werden sich die Schutzrechte noch stärker ausdehnen und manifestieren, insbesondere auch die Durchsetzung und Verfolgung der Nutzungsrechte. Die amerikanische Musikindustrie beginnt ja bereits private Peer-to-Peer-Netzwerknutzer zivil- und strafrechtlich zu verfolgen. Und das wird nur der Anfang sein. Für den Verbraucher wird dies bedeuten, dass er sämtliches Datenmaterial künftig nur noch gegen Geld erhält. Für die Urheber wird dies eine Verbesserung des Urheberrechtsschutzes und damit die Sicherung ihrer Einkünfte bedeuten.

⇛ Rechtsanwalt Jens Olaf Brelle, Alter Wandrahm 15,
D-20457 Hamburg-Speicherstadt, www.art-lawyer.de

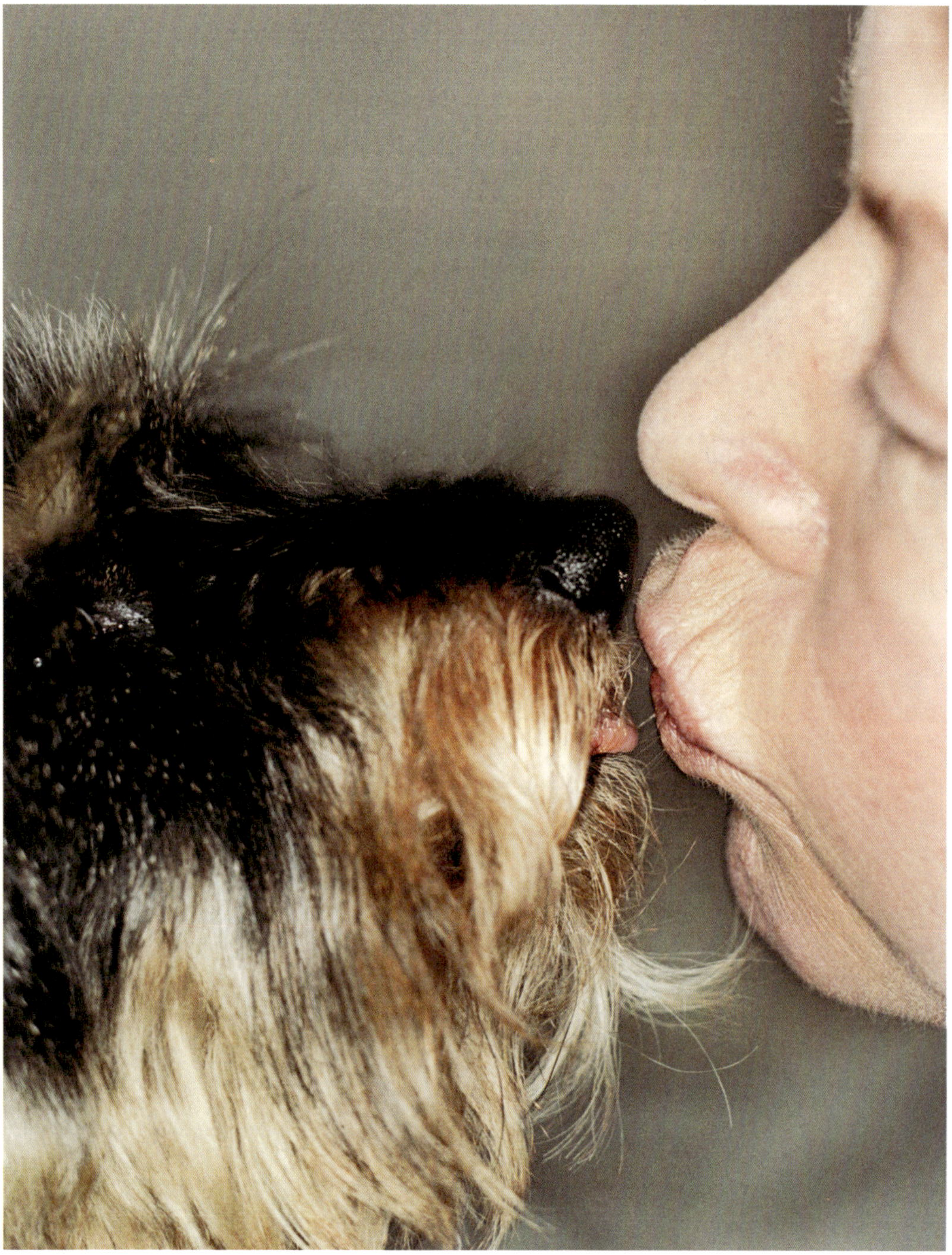

Dogs, not diamonds, are a girl's best friend

PHOTOGRAPHY BY
SUSANNE WALSTRÖM _LUNDLUND.COM

WORDS BY
FELIX SCHWENZEL _M-PUBLICATION.COM/WIRRES

STYLING _MAGNUS FLOBECKER
HAIR AND MAKE UP _MAGDA. MODELS _CHRISTINA AND BIBBI

"A kiss makes the heart young again and wipes out the years." *Rupert Brooke*

Gemäß Paragraph 1, Absatz 1, Satz 4 des Fleischhygienegesetzes ist der Verzehr von Hundefleisch in Deutschland verboten. Trotz der vom Fleischhygienegesetz angemahnten Fleischhygiene darf man Hunde in Deutschland nach belieben küssen. So viel man will. Auch auf den Mund. Pardon, die Schnauze. Allerdings raten nicht nur Tierärzte von übermäßigem Mund-Schnauze-Kontakt ab, auch der gesunde Menschenverstand sollte dies tun. Schließlich sind Hunde sehr gelenkig und können daher mit ihrer Zunge Dinge tun, von denen die Menschheit schon seit Adam und Eva träumt.

Wen das nicht schreckt, wer aber Anstoß am schlechten Atem des zu küssenden Hundes nimmt, für den gibt es auch eine Mundpflege-Serie namens Dog-A-Dent. Dog-A-Dent gibt es – ganz undekadent – als Zahnpasta mit Zahnbürste, als Maulspray oder als Kau-Tabs, gegen Mundgeruch, Karies und Zahnbelag.

Wer sich trotz Mundhygiene nicht an die feuchten Stellen des Hundes traut, kann trotzdem profitieren: Schmusen oder auch nur das Kraulen des Hundenackens senkt nachweislich den Blutdruck des Kraulers. Auch gegen Schmerzen sei das Tierkraulen wirksam, berichtet die Deutsche Schmerzliga.

Es ist unbestritten – das Zusammenleben mit einem Hund hat eine positive therapeutische Wirkung auf den Hundebesitzer. Außerdem strukturiert ein Hund den

Tagesablauf des Menschen und ersetzt damit auch oftmals den fehlenden Partner.

Die Redewendung "auf den Hund gekommen" spielt beispielsweise darauf an, dass es älteren oder verwitweten Frauen nicht nur an Geld mangeln würde, sondern speziell am Partner, so dass sie, auch als Triebbefriedigung, "auf den Hund kommen".

Ebenso ist die Herkunft des Begriffs "Schoßhündchen" auf seine Funktion als Triebbefriediger im Schoß seines Frauchens zurückzuführen. Der Schoßhund ist also eine Art vorindustrieller Vibrator-Ersatz, gelegentlich auch "Punzenlecker" genannt.

Heutzutage dient ein Hund aber auch, wissenschaftlich nachweisbar, zur Anbahnung von Sozialkontakten, sozusagen als "Kontaktagent". Angeblich sind bereits 70 Prozent aller Hundebesitzer schon einmal einem anderen Menschen via Hund näher gekommen. Solcherlei Kontaktanbahnung via Rüde/Hündin kann man aber auch mit einem "Rüden-Abwehr-Zerstäuber" verhindern, der – regelmäßig angewendet – den Lockstoff der Hündin neutralisiert.

Ein Hund kann seinem Halter aber auch ein gewisse Prise Glamour verleihen: Eine Untersuchung der TU Berlin konnte einen statistischen Zusammenhang zwischen einem Faible für schöne Autos oder elegante Wohnungen und einer Vorliebe für schöne und auffallende (Rasse-)Hunde herstellen.

OrderforM

M Publication – Collector's Edition

· 210 x 270 mm, 208 pages, 4 colours, 900 g
· plus additional special colours and engraving techniques
· different paper qualities, 100-400 g/m^2
· numbered and limited to 3,000 copies worldwide
· plus additional editorials of 16 pages
· special packaging and gift

Volume 02 is enhanced by a bag designed by the Strenesse chief designer Gabriele Strehle. Schwan-Stabilo has created a Stabilo 's move pen specially for this edition.

M Publication VOLUME	Collector's Edition PRE-ORDER	Regular Edition REPEAT ORDER
01 Power	__ 17 Euro	__ 13 Euro
02 Luxury	__ 26 Euro	__ 17 Euro
03 Surprise	__ 26 Euro	__ 17 Euro
04 Tomorrow	__ 26 Euro	__ 17 Euro

Plus a fixed dispatch fee of: 5 Euro (Germany) / 12 Euro (Europe) / 25 Euro (rest of world). M Publication is sent by airmail.

MY ADDRESS

First name	Last name
Profession	Company
Street / no.	ZIP / City
Country	Date of birth
Telephone	Telefax
Email	

PAYMENT METHOD __ Direct debit __ Credit card

Sort code	Bank	Account no.
Credit card no.		Expiry date

Date, 1st signature

Right to revocation: The order can be cancelled within ten days at the order address. Cancellation of the order must follow in good time in order to adhere to the revocation period. I confirm these details with my signature. I consent to my name, communication data, bank details and debit amounts being saved (electronically) for sales purposes. The personal data provided here will not be forwarded to a third party.

Date, 2nd signature

Fax to: +49.69.801069.10 // www.M-Publication.com

ARDI GOLDMAN. MAY 2003 – AT HOME, FRANKFURT.
PHOTOGRAPHY BY DARIUS RAMAZANI. ASSISTANT: HAMILTON PEREIRA. LABOR: OPAQUE BERLIN, PIETRO GIRIBALDI.

Alles hat seinen Preis

Visionäre sehen das, was andere nicht sehen können. Ardi Goldman über Fata Morgana, seine Heimatstadt Frankfurt und wahren Luxus.

Wie definierst du Luxus?
_Luxus ist das, was man sich nicht leisten kann, und das, was man gerade nicht besitzt. Luxus ist abhängig von der persönlichen Begriffsdefinition – ein Surfer z. B., der leidenschaftlich gerne surft, empfindet Wellenreiten als das größte Luxuserlebnis. Dafür verzichtet er wohl auf andere Dinge. Andere dagegen wollen lieber ein Schloss in Schottland besitzen oder einen Luxusoldtimer fahren. Luxus ist gleichzusetzen mit Lebensgefühl, sich selbst einen Lebenstraum zu erfüllen, egal in welcher Weise.

Auf was könntest du verzichten?
_Ich besitze nichts Wertvolleres als meine Erinnerungen und meinen Erfahrungsschatz, die mich geprägt haben und zu dem gemacht haben, was ich bin.

Wie wichtig ist Geld?
_Geld spielt eine unabdingbare Rolle. Ohne Geld kein Luxus, denn alles hat seinen Preis.

Bestimmt der Preis, ob etwas luxuriös ist?
_Luxus ist ein gemachtes Gut. Ein Gut wird verknappt, dadurch steigt der Preis künstlich in die Höhe. Es wird etwas suggeriert, was gar nicht wahr ist. Luxus ist eine Suggestion von Wünschen. Diese Mechanismen kenne ich und suche daher die Qualität, wenn ich mit hohen Preisen konfrontiert werde. Die Modewelt ist eine Fata Morgana.

Sind die Leute neidisch auf dich?
_Luxus provoziert Neid. Wir entwickeln uns immer mehr zu einem Sozialistenstaat. Reichtum für alle, Kapitalismus für alle. Allerdings will es keiner wahr haben, dass Wohlstand für alle nicht Sache des Staates ist, sondern jedes Einzelnen. Ein großer Unterschied zu den Amerikanern. Dort ist die Möglichkeit, es vom Tellerwäscher zum Millionär zu schaffen, viel größer. Die Parameter Arbeit, soziale Gerechtigkeit und Wohlstand stimmen momentan bei uns in Deutschland nicht überein und entwickeln sich in eine merkwürdige Richtung.

Musst du arbeiten?
_Für viele andere ist das Arbeiten ein notwendiges Mittel. Ich muss nicht arbeiten, aber ich bin in der glücklichen Lage, dass ich meine Arbeit liebe und meine Verwirklichung darin sehe. Meine Arbeit ist für mich schöpferisch – wie für einen Künstler. Ich produziere und schaffe etwas. Hauche sozusagen Leben in ein Produkt ein. Daher ist meine Arbeit für mich Luxus, weil ich mit meiner Arbeit nicht nur Geld verdiene, sondern darauf auch Lust habe.

Viele ziehen nach Berlin, du auch?
_Ich will nicht nach Berlin. Frankfurt ist ein großes Dorf. Gerade dieses Merkmal macht die Stadt auch angenehm und liebenswert für mich. Frankfurt ist meine Basis und mein Zuhause. Ich kann zusehen, wie sich die Stadt verändert. Mit der Stadt verbinde ich diverse Erinnerungen und habe eine spezielle unerklärliche Bindung, ich kenne jeden Winkel und fühle mich hier zugehörig.

Was bedeutet dir Frankfurt?
_Ich wohne hier und arbeite hier: ein Geben und ein Nehmen. Es laufen aktuell diverse Projekte, wie der Portikus, das UFO und das Stadtwerk. Ich glaube mit meiner Arbeit hinterlasse ich schon meine Spuren. Die Individualität in allen Bereichen zu fördern und beizubehalten ist wichtig für mich und für die Entwicklung Frankfurts.

Frankfurt im Vergleich zu anderen Weltstädten?
_Frankfurt ist auf den ersten Blick keine glamouröse Stadt. Aber wenn man in den diversen Stadtteilen wie Bornheim, Nordend, Sachsenhausen oder auf der Hanauer Landstraße nach Luxus sucht, kann man die Vorzüge einer "kleinen" Stadt genießen und trotzdem fündig werden. Andere Städte sind zu groß, um rasch und bequem erschlossen zu werden. Alle Projekte, an denen ich arbeite oder arbeiten will, dienen dazu, den Luxusfaktor für die Stadt Frankfurt zu erhöhen. Luxus ist nämlich eine Frage des Angebots. Und die Nachfrage bestimmt das Angebot. Tagsüber ist Frankfurt sehr aktiv und nachts kann es nicht mit den anderen Städten mithalten. Zwei Millionen Menschen sind tagsüber hier, und nachts verschwinden sie. Das will ich ändern.

Denkst du auch mal an das Aufhören?
Viele träumen von der "Sabbatical Break". Ich erachte eine solche Pause aber als heimtückisch. Wenn man sie antritt, lodert das Feuer des Schaffens wieder auf und man will gleich wieder arbeiten. Auf der anderen Seite ist Zeit sowieso eins der größten Luxusgüter. Sie ist knapp und man hat nicht viel davon. Wer kann sich schon drei Monate Urlaub leisten? Ich nicht. /////

⇛ Goldman Holding, Carl-Benz-Str. 35, D-60386 Frankfurt
T. +49.69.947413.0, www.goldman-holding.de

Valkoi

People said that computer technology was supposed to replace paper. They were absolutely wrong. Paper will always remain the physical embodiment of information. Paper piles are living and breathing archives for innumerable ideas and as long as we are humans, we will depend on paper and ink to nourish our senses.

Creating white luxury

Impressions of the M-real papermill, Stockstadt, Germany

Valkoinen kulta is finnish and means white gold

BY KIMBERLY LLOYD

Commercialising is the game

BandK, an austrialian duo, on obstacles in the music industry and the myriad possibilities of the Internet.

What is BandK?
_Blaine: BandK is anything and everything. BandK is a mixture of things. A mixture of the good, the clean, the dirty and the fun. For both of us, music is a natural way of expressing ourselves, just like someone else might paint, write, whatever. Our music is not calculated music. But if we have to describe it, BandK's music is a collection of the rhythms and melodies that have been running around in our heads since we were children. To get into genre nitty-gritty, it's part house, part indie guitar, part electro and lots of fun. We like the idea of our music being used for a range of purposes, projects and applications, some of them being artistic and self-indulgent.

When performing on stage, BandK is more elaborate in the usage of multimedia. Why do you choose these visual elements to interact with, influence and accentuate your tracks?
_Krathyn: For BandK, imagery is vital because it's an extension of the music. It creates feeling, mood and atmosphere, and magnifies the immediacy – a collision of ideas manifested through music and sound. Sometimes the imagery is obviously connected to the music but other times the connection is more conceptual. This is something we see as important across the board, whether it's our record sleeves, live visual projections or our website.

Numerous artists distribute their tracks at the blink of an eye on the Internet. No more administrative work, no more A&R barriers. Que sera sera?
_Krathyn: It's imperative that artists and musicians keep an open mind about accessibility and distribution, and it's this very issue which means musicians and artists have to have an open mind in terms of the commercialising they do.

Some artists are careful of commercialising or selling out their work. The limitation of their music to a small crowd at a club means a lot more to them than signing a contract with a major label.
_Krathyn: The fear of commercialisation and selling out when it comes to music is kind of tiresome. It isn't necessarily a bad thing. Commercialising might sound like a pretty hardcore capitalist idea, but it's the reality and a means to an end and something that can be controlled. We want the world to hear our music and we make it for people to enjoy – it's not a cliquey thing or something that's meant to be elitist. Commercialising what we do would mean that we can quit our day jobs and dedicate ourselves completely to our passion. And like most things in life, commercialising is a game you have to learn to play to your advantage and not be taken advantage of.

_Blaine: Look at someone like Björk who has successfully commercialised her music and managed to do exactly what she wants, using her artistic power to almost subvert her own commercialisation by working with some of the most prestigious underground artists. Who else would have the ability to get artists like Matmos, Console and Opiate to remix their work as well as sampling artists like Oval on albums that go on to sell millions?

What is next?
_Krathyn: We are in the midst of planning a fully immersive multimedia event, tentatively titled AvSex-System, to be staged later this year in Sydney. It's an idea that tries to play with the notion of multimedia and be more than music with pretty pictures. The idea is to create a fucked-up cabaret of sorts that includes live painting, performance art, dance and whatever else springs to mind. We're working on this idea with other like-minded artists in Sydney who share this philosophy. You see people pushing the idea of multimedia but a lot of it seems lacking in the multi part.

Blaine, apart from composing music for BandK, you also engineer and produce the material. Why does this side of making music appeal to you?
_Composition is only half the story when creating a track. Have you ever listened to CDs or records and thought, hey, this sounds bigger and louder, or has a great sound quality that you can't quite put your finger on compared to other CDs you listen to? Production is like giving a track a bigger personality to stand up and be heard. Not to say that a track with little production hasn't got a personality. It's making what's there more special and pronounced. There's a lot of satisfaction in making what you have written sound fucking amazing. Whenever I listen to a track produced by one of my favourite producers, I love to deconstruct it in my head and think, how is that done, and bring some of those feelings, as well as my own, to the final sound of BandK. /////

⇒ www.bandkmusik.com
✚ See Krathyn White's short story on page 66.
Listen to BandK: www.M-Publication.com

Presidential Suite

PHOTOGRAPHY BY
TXEMA YESTE

BY KIMBERLY LLOYD

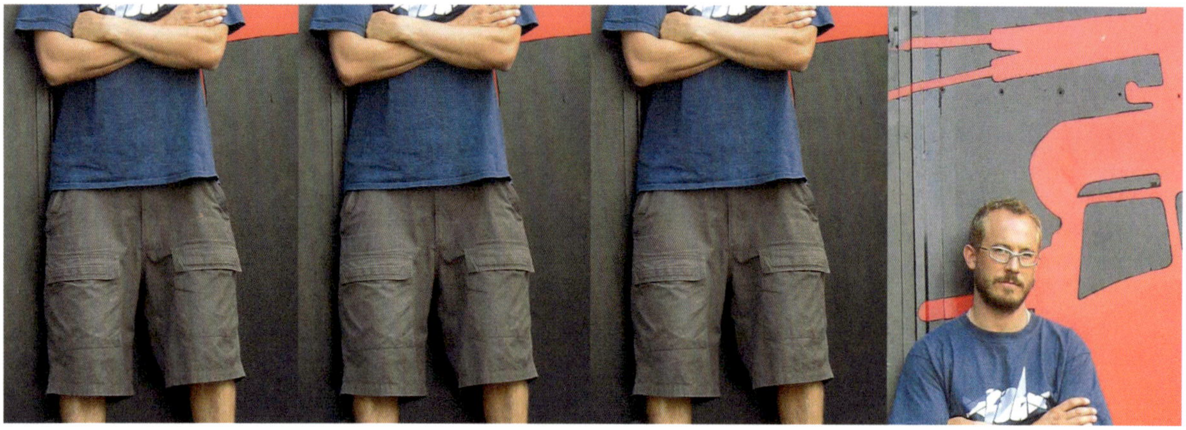

To roll or not to roll

It is not only the inside of the bag that reveals our wealth, status and character, but also the outside of it. Our possessions rule our lives and our minds. Protecting and transporting our riches is of main significance. Simon Nicholls on transporting personal belongings in a bag.

PHOTOGRAPHY BY
THOMAS REINER

What are the main functions of a bag for you?
_Mainly to carry my life from A to B. In the last 18 months, I have clocked a quarter of a million air miles. When you travel that much there is no distinction between night and day, work or play. There is just life, and I carry mine on my back.

List of your properties and price tag your belongings.
_Personally I carry enough electronics to liberate a small country, more megahertz than can be legally imported into the Middle East. I have my laptop, an iPod, a PDA, a digicam, mobile phones, a terminal case, a Maglite, multiple cables and chargers, stickers and a book. I don't know how much I have spent, but definitely quite a lot.

Anything to know about the outside of a bag?
_The outside should be "dope". The inside should be "Zen" like tranquillity, balance and harmony.

What does the content reveal?
_First of all, the bag itself reveals the most; I mean there is more to it than just the bag you take to work or school, or the handbag you dance around. Bags are a true mix of fashion and function. You can have backpacks, shoulder bags, tote purses and shoppers; but a whole other world exists around product-specific luggage, for example surfboard bags, snowboard bags, skate packs, bike bags, golf bags. This can give you a clue to someone's interests ... these are often used in conjunction with travel bags which are really starting to evolve. To roll or not to roll is the current issue dilemma. In the same way that someone carrying a matching set of monogrammed chests can be stereotyped, so can the guy in the suit running the Burton day hiker. There are all sorts of clues to look for, from the design, to the age, to the brand and what they run it with.

No excuses of not being able to find the key again because the Gravis luggage is systemised to the maximum. What made the Gravis designers arrange this chaos?
_Every year, Gravis spends thousands of dollars kitting out team riders with luggage; the riders get their products for free, so without any value than to transport their stuff. They travel all over the world, snow, desert and beaches, luggage gets trashed and if the bag does not fit their purposes, riders will not continue to use it. Therefore we have to make our products perform better for the user. This is part of our continual product evolution. Over the years, this has developed into an art form which we pass on to the consumer at every available opportunity.

What does the term luxury mean to you?
_The ability to sleep in my own bed and take a shower in the morning. /////

Simon Nicholls
Born in the United Kingdom, on 8th Nov 1973, is a passionate surfer, snowboarder. Simon is the marketing director for Gravis and the brand director Gravis-Analog.

⇛ Gravis Europe, Haller Strasse 111, A-6020 Innsbruck
T. +43.512205500, www.gravisfootwear.com

Einmal atmen 3,00 Euro

(Dreimal 7,50 Euro) Den Luxus leist' ich mir.

PHOTOGRAPHY BY
PIERO BORSELLINO

WORDS BY
THOMAS FEICHT

Kommunikation geht schon manchmal verwirrende Wege. Ist das nun eine Coop-Aktion für Freiheit und Abenteuer oder der Weg aus der verrauchten, erstickenden Welt der Städte? Aber versetzen wir uns doch kurz nach New York. Als Raucher. Sitzend im Rinnstein, am Straßenrand – der Rest der Freiheit, die geblieben ist. Hören wir nun auf zu rauchen oder fahren wir in die Schweiz und werfen unsere Stummel in die Landschaft (wo sie einige 100 Jahre zum Verrotten brauchen) oder langt uns diese Illusion als Ersatzurlaub? Oder ist das Ganze ein Testmarkt. Marlboro bereitet ein neues Produkt vor. Bergluft in Zigarettenpackung (Preis siehe oben).

Thomas Feicht
Frager und Sprecher des Vorstandes beim Deutschen Designer Club (DDC)
und Nachdenker und Schreiber bei TRUST in Communication, Frankfurt am Main.

M Publication – board of contributors

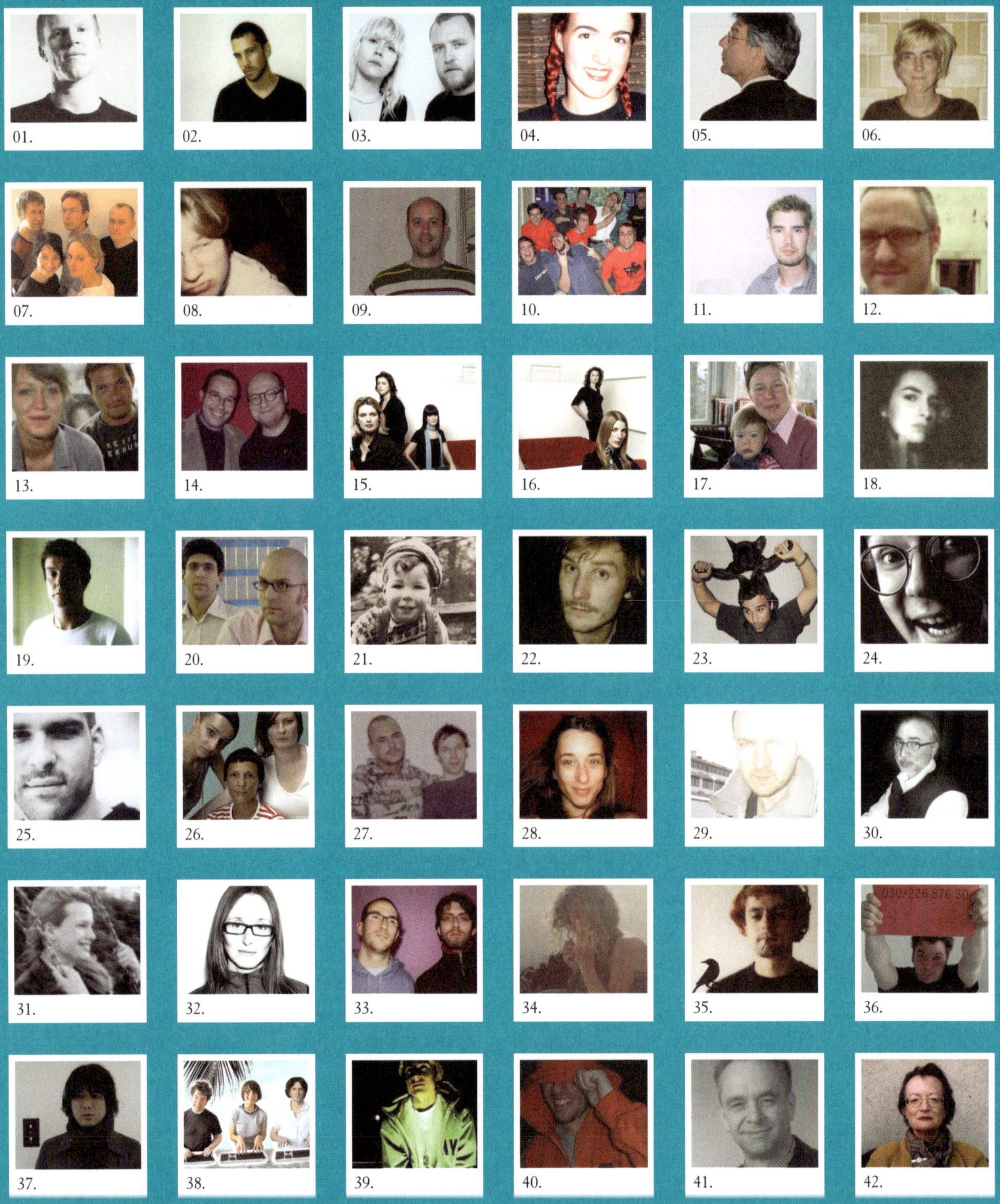

M strongly encourages contributors to join the publication for the upcoming volumes.
How to contribute? www.M-Publication.com

01. Krathyn White	Author & musician	Australia	www.bandkmusik.com
02. Johann Hähling von Lanzenauer	Creative director	Germany	www.circleculture.com
03. Lyn Balzer & Tony Perkins	Photographer	Australia	lynbtonyp@ozemail.com.au
04. Leila Mendez	Photographer	Spain	www.leilamendez.com
05. Michael Miersch	Author	Germany	www.maxeiner-miersch.de
06. Sabine Schründer	Photographer	Germany	www.foto-union.de
07. Friedrichs & Friends	Proof reading	Germany	www.friedrichsfriends.de
08. Jonas Banker	Illustrator	Sweden	www.agentform.se
09. Jörg Skalecki	Author	Germany	joerg.skalecki@gmx.de
10. Vasava	Designers	Spain	www.vasava.es
11. Nico Hesselmann	Photographer	Germany	www.foto-union.de
12. Rudi Beckmann	Designer	Germany	www.diegestalten.de
13. Fotounion	Representatives	Germany	www.foto-union.de
14. Just.Burgeff	Architects	Germany	www.just.burgeff.de
15. LundLund	Representatives	Sweden	www.lundlund.com
16. Lundlund	Representatives	Sweden	www.lundlund.com
17. Agentform	Representatives	Sweden	www.agentform.se
18. Sally Gross	Manager	England	www.gotanproject.com
19. Marcel Meury	Photographer	Germany	www.foto-union.de
20. Visuarte	Designers	Germany	www.visuarte.de
21. Robin Preston	Postproductioner	Germany	www.kombinatrotweiss.de
22. Dirk Staudinger	Creative director	Germany	www.circleculture.de
23. Txema Yeste	Photographer	Spain	www.txyeste.com
24. Axel Thomae	Photographer	Germany	www.kombinatrotweiss.de
25. Darius Ramazani	Photographer	Germany	www.ramazani.de
26. Kombinatrotweiss	Representatives	Germany	www.kombinatrotweiss.de
27. Andreas Johansson	Photographer	Sweden	www.lundlund.com
Lars Fredrik Svedberg	Stylist	Sweden	www.lundlund.com
28. Prisca Lobjoy	Video artist	France	www.gotanproject.com
29. Dominik Gigler	Photographer	England	www.klosslondon.com
30. Thomas Feicht	Author	Germany	www.trust.de
31. Julia Grossi	Photographer	Germany	www.juliagrossi.com
32. Susanne Walström	Photographer	Sweden	www.lundlund.com
33. Subakt	Designers	France	www.subakt.fr
34. Sam Kloss	Representative	England	www.klosslondon.com
35. Arnaud Mercier	Designer	France	www.elixirstudio.com
36. Felix Schwenzel	Author	Germany	www.wirres.net
37. Takeshi Hamada	Designer	Japan	www.tigermagazine.org
38. Panatom	Developer	Germany	www.panatom.de
39. Alexander Schukowski	Illustrator	Germany	kombinatdesigns@aol.com
40. Marok	Designer	Germany	www.lodown.de
41. Prof. Dr. Klaus Mainzer	Author	Germany	University Augsburg
42. Margit Gaudard	Author	Switzerland	./.
43. Swedengraphics	Designers	Sweden	www.swedengraphics.com

ZEIT SPAREN MIT INSTANT PRODUKTEN, WIE DIE »FÜNF-MINUTEN-TERRINE«
UND DEM TÜRKISCHEN BABYBREI »ARI – EKONOMIK BOY«. WWW.M-PUBLICATION.COM/M-SHOP

Zeit ist unser kostbarstes Gut

Zeit ist knapp und daher ein kostbares Gut. Sie läuft ab und scheint dabei einem ehernen Gesetz zu gehorchen: Wir werden geboren, wachsen, altern und sterben. Unsere Lebenszeit hat eine Richtung. Aber auch in unseren Kulturen und Zivilisationen scheinen Ordnungen von Städten, Staaten und Gesellschaften ebenso zu entstehen, zu reifen und zu zerfallen wie in der Natur. Der Ein-druck des Zeitpfeils beschränkt sich also nicht nur auf die biologische Evolution. Nach den Gesetzen der Phy-sik könnten allerdings auch alle Uhren rückwärts laufen.

Kein Physiker wird aber bestreiten, dass eine biologische Zeitrichtung bereits durch die Abfolge von Generationen gegeben ist: Eltern, Großeltern, Urgroßeltern etc. bestimmen die Vergangenheit, Kinder und Kindeskinder die Zukunft. In Darwins Evolutionstheorie geht es nicht nur um die Abfolge von Generationen einer Art, sondern um die zeitliche Abfolge von Arten, die auseinander entstanden sind. Zeitliche Abfolgen und Verzweigungen der Arten aus gemeinsamen Vorgängern lassen sich heute durch Veränderungen von Gensequenzen bestimmen. Aus genetischen Verwandtschaftsgraden ergeben sich komplexe Entwicklungsmuster mit Brüchen und Verwerfungen. Die Evolution ist ein Kampf um Lebenszeit.

Zelluläre Organismen sind Beispiele von komplexen Systemen, deren Zustände durch die Wechselwirkungen ihrer vielen Elemente bestimmt sind. Gase und Flüssigkeiten bestehen aus vielen Molekülen, Organismen aus Zellen und Organen, Populationen aus Individuen, die unterschiedliche zeitliche Entwicklungen durchlaufen. Der Gesamtzustand des komplexen Systems bezieht sich daher nur auf die Mittelung von statistischen Verteilungsfunktionen individueller Zustände. Ihre Entwicklung strebt nach dem zweiten Hauptsatz der Thermodynamik Gleichgewichtszuständen zu, deren zeitliche Umkehrung extrem unwahrscheinlich ist. Daher wurde vorgeschlagen, Zeit nicht nur als Abfolge von Zahlenwerten auf einer Uhr ("Zeitparameter") zu verstehen, sondern als Entwicklung von Verteilungsfunktionen, die durch einen Zeitoperator bestimmt ist. Man unterscheidet daher zwischen der "äußeren" Parameterzeit, die sich auf einer Uhr außerhalb und unabhängig von der Entwicklung eines Systems ablesen lässt, und der "inneren" Operatorzeit, die das durchschnittliche "Alter" eines Systems zum Ausdruck bringt. Ein Fünfzigjähriger kann Herz und Kreislauf eines Vierzigjährigen, als Leistungssportler aber die verschlissenen Gelenke und Sehnen eines Siebzigjährigen haben. Organe, Arterien, Knochen und Muskeln sind in verschiedenen Zuständen, die unterschiedlichen Lebensbedingungen und genetischen Dispositionen entsprechen. Häufig kündigen sich Krankheiten durch gestörte innere Zeitrhythmen an: Wenn wir die beschleunigte Zellteilung eines lokalen Krebstumors bemerken, ist es meistens zu spät. Nur das mittlere Alter unseres gesamten Körpers wächst im gleichen Maß wie die verstreichende äußere Uhrzeit.

Auch das menschliche Gehirn lässt sich als komplexes System verstehen, in dem viele Neuronen und Areale chemisch wechselwirken. Sie verschalten sich selbständig in Verteilungsmustern, die unseren Gefühlen oder Gedanken entsprechen. Wenn glückliche Erlebnisse "wie im Flug" vorübergehen und Stress- und Angstzustände "eine Ewigkeit" zu dauern scheinen, dann entsprechen diese subjektiven Eindrücke komplexen Gehirnzuständen, die von vielen individuellen Umständen und Dispositionen abhängen. Zeitdruck und Zeitbeschleunigung können uns aber auch krank machen. Medizin und Gehirnforschung kennen zwar noch nicht alle Details. Jedenfalls stehen subjektive Zeitempfindung und naturwissenschaftliche Zeitkonzepte nicht im Gegensatz.

Die innere Zeit komplexer Systeme lässt sich auch in der Dynamik menschlicher Gesellschaften nachweisen. Institutionen, Betriebe und Verwaltungen entwickeln ihre eigenen Zeitrhythmen. Unternehmen kämpfen um Produktionszeiten, um ihre Produkte marktgerecht zu platzieren. Arbeitszeiten führen zu tariflichen Auseinandersetzungen. Städte wachsen wie Organismen: In einer Stadt wie Rom leben verschiedene Zeit- und Stilepochen von der Antike bis zur Moderne mit unterschiedlichen Entwicklungsrhythmen nebeneinander. Rom im Jahr 2002 bezieht sich auf das Durchschnittsalter eines urbanen Systems, das sich in komplexen Siedlungsmustern zeigt. In den Metropolen dieser Erde spüren wir auch den "Puls der Zeit". Das ist aber nicht die Uhr- und Kalenderzeit. Der Jahrtausendwechsel des Jahres 2000 blieb ein numerisches Ereignis, ohne tief greifende Spuren für die Menschheit zu hinterlassen. Der 11. September 2001 in New York veränderte aber die globale Entwicklung. Nur scheinbar handelte es sich um eine Zufallszahl. Viele kleine vorherige Ereignisse und Erschütterungen haben dieses Erdbeben vorbereitet. Aber wir haben sie nicht bemerkt. Bereits in Geographie und Geologie lassen sich in einer Landschaft vielschichtige Muster von Gebirgen, Gesteinssegmentierungen und Verwerfungen aus unterschiedlichen Epochen angeben. Darauf bezieht sich das durchschnittliche Erdzeitalter. Auch das Alter des Universums lässt sich aus Verteilungsmustern vom heißen uniformen Urzustand bis zu komplexen galaktischen Strukturen ablesen. Kosmische Erschütterungen von der Geburt neuer Sterne bis zum Kollaps schwarzer Löcher bereiten sich unbemerkt aus dem Zusammenwirken unzähliger Ereignisse vor. Die äußere Uhrzeit weiß davon nichts. Wir sollten daher weniger geschäftig auf die Uhr schauen und statt dessen sensibel werden für die inneren Zeitrhythmen von Natur und Gesellschaft.

- The Little Book of Time, Prof. Dr. K. Mainzer, Copernicus
- www.springer.de
- Respond&Win. Lob und Tadel.
  M verschenkt 5 Exemplare des o.g. Buches.
  WinTime@M-Publication.com
  Einsendeschluss: 30.11.2003. Der Rechtsweg ist ausgeschlossen.

You don't know what you've got until it's gone.

Du hast nur eine Mama und einen Papa.

PHOTOGRAPHY BY
JÜRGEN TELLER

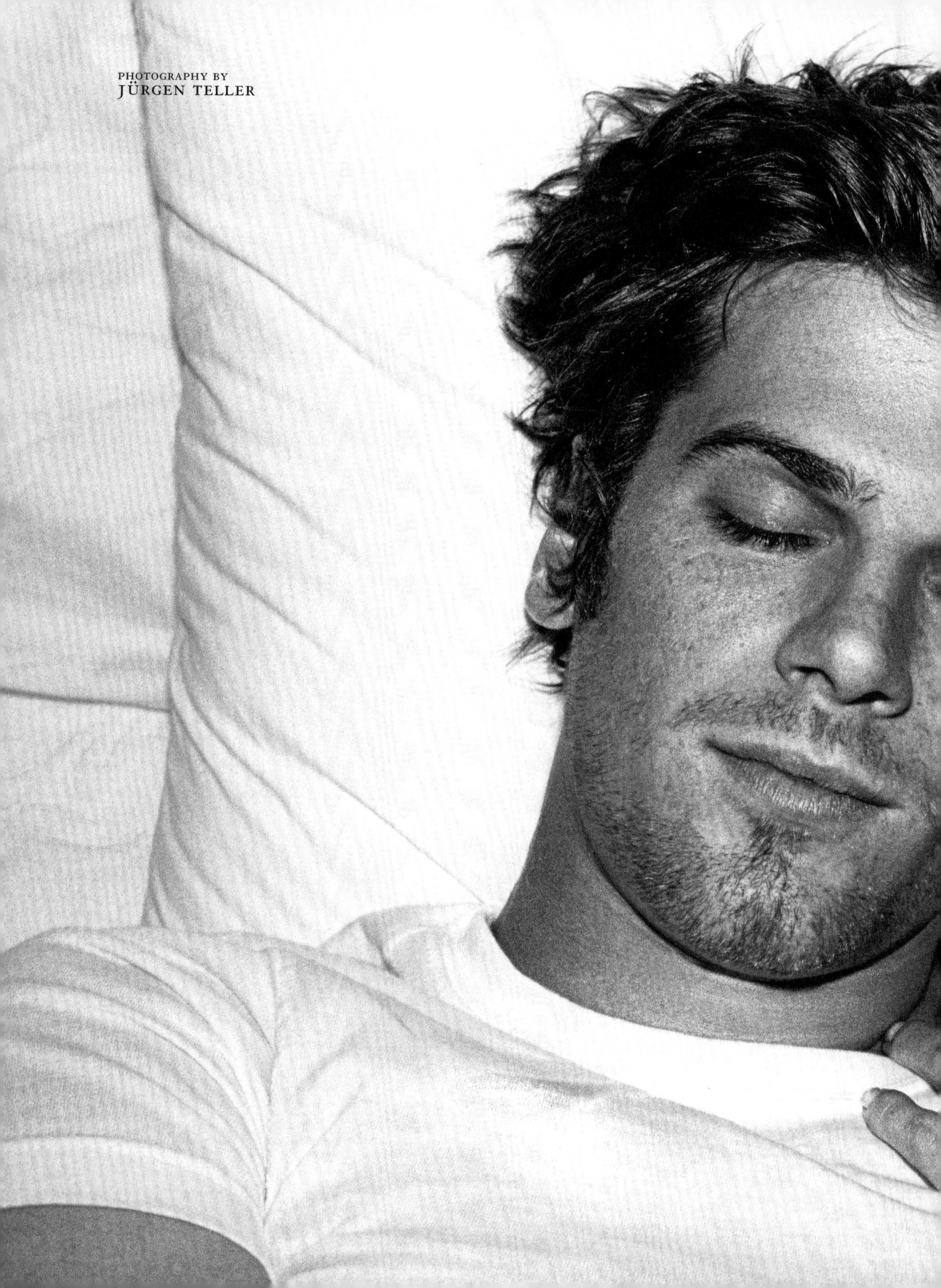

ETERNITY
for men
Calvin Klein
ETERNITY
Calvin Klein